GW00641906

Christmas Pictures

*Devotional thoughts
for Christmas*

Roger Ellsworth

BRYNTIRION PRESS

© Roger Ellsworth, 2010

First published 2010

ISBN 978 1 85049 239 9

Biblical quotations are taken from the British usage text of
The Holy Bible, New King James Version
© Thomas Nelson, Inc., 1982

Cover design: Creative Media Publishing Limited

Published by Bryntirion Press,
Bryntirion, Bridgend CF31 4DX, Wales

Printed in Wales by Gomer Press, Llandysul, Ceredigion, SA44 4JL

Christmas
Pictures

Contents

Introduction

Each Christmas season finds me casting about for devotional material that will help me to stand in awe of the truths that Christmas celebrates.

It is my hope that these chapters will help bring that awe to others.

My purpose is not to break new ground, but rather to make old ground new. While we Christians understand the meaning of Christmas, we do not always feel the glory of it to the degree that we should. It is not enough in a sceptical and unbelieving world to merely state the facts. Only a sense of awe and wonder will fuel deep devotion to Christ and energetic service for his kingdom.

And one cannot help but wonder if that sense of wonder is a crucial ingredient for Christians to share their faith effectively in a sceptical and unbelieving world. It should be painfully clear to us that it is possible to win the argument without winning the unbeliever. It is not enough to merely state the facts about Christmas. We must, by the grace of God, show that those facts have made a positive difference to us.

If God is pleased to use these chapters to such ends, I will be grateful.

Roger Ellsworth, January 2010

Section 1

A woman, a child
and a dragon

1.
The dragon and the expectant woman

Read: Revelation 12:1-6

I am always happy to see the Christmas season arrive. I enjoy the beautiful decorations. I love the Christmas music. I delight in the warm greetings of family members and friends. But the primary reason I rejoice in Christmas is that it calls us to think deeply and seriously about the greatness of our salvation.

Each Christmas season we hear people talking about what Christmas is 'all about'. The Christian knows what Christmas is about. Christmas is about Christ. It is about him coming to this world in our humanity and living and dying on our behalf so that our sins can be forgiven and we can have a home in heaven.

Christmas, then, is about God's plan of redemption. This is, of course, the great theme of the Bible. The Bible is a book about redemption. It is about man losing his paradise through sin and God restoring that paradise through grace.

This Christmas season let us explore again the wonders of redemption, and we will begin to do so by drawing upon the book of Revelation. There is, of course, no more controversial book in the Bible. Is the book of Revelation a book exclusively about the past or is it a book exclusively about the future? My answer to that question is that it is not exclusively a book about either. It is about both. We have here in Revelation a description of what the people of God have experienced in every age, what they are experiencing now, and what they will continue to experience, with greater intensity, at the end.

With that principle in mind, we approach this twelfth chapter. Here we have God's plan of redemption put to us in a particularly powerful way. It is presented in terms of a drama that

11

has been working its way out all through human history and will continue to do so until the end.

This drama consists primarily of three characters on the stage of human history: a woman, a child and a dragon.

There is no difficulty in determining who two of these characters are intended to represent. Verse 5 tells us that the child 'was to rule all nations with a rod of iron' and would be 'caught up to God and to his throne'. The child is, then, none other than the Lord Jesus Christ. Verse 9 is equally clear about the dragon: 'So the great dragon was cast out, that serpent of old, called the Devil and Satan, who deceives the whole world.'

That brings us to the woman. Who is she? This passage tells us several things about her. First, we are told that she was beautiful and glorious. The apostle John, the author of Revelation, describes her as 'a woman clothed with the sun, with the moon under her feet, and on her head a garland of twelve stars' (v.1). Secondly, we are told that she 'cried out in labour and in pain to give birth' (v.2). Thirdly, we are told that the dragon, Satan, sought to devour her child (v.4). The phrase 'as soon as it was born' focuses our attention on Satan's activity the night Christ was born, but, as we shall have occasion to note, Satan worked long and hard before Christ was born, seeking to make it impossible for him to be born. Finally, we are told that the woman bore the child (v.5), after which she fled into the wilderness to a place prepared for her by God.

It is obvious that this woman is not intended to represent Mary. While she was indeed the mother of Jesus, she does not fit all the elements of the description we have here. The final part of the description is enough to make that clear. There is something going on here that is much larger and greater than Mary. We can do justice to this description only if we identify the woman as a depiction of the people of God.

We have identified the child as Christ, the dragon as Satan and the woman as the people of God. We are ready, therefore, to deal with the great drama in which these characters participate. It is the drama of Christmas.

The antagonistic dragon

This one, whom we know as Satan, has quite a CV. He first steps on to the stage of human history in Genesis 3 in order to bring Adam and Eve into rebellion against God. But Satan did not begin to exist with human history. He had a long history already before he ever appeared in Genesis 3. He was originally one of God's angels, perhaps the greatest of all the angels. His name was Lucifer.

Created for the purpose of serving God and bringing glory to God, Lucifer was filled with pride. In his pride, he led one-third of all the angels (v.4) in rebellion against God (Isa. 14:12-14). The rebellion failed (as is the case with all rebellion against God), and Lucifer and his band of angels were cast out of heaven.

From that time forward, Lucifer became Satan, which means 'adversary'. Since his failed rebellion Satan has been on a course of opposition to God. Unable to dethrone God in heaven, he has tried to defeat God on earth. Frederick S. Leahy writes of Satan: 'Having lost a crown in heaven, Satan now endeavored to establish a throne on earth, in man's heart. That is the story of Genesis 3.'[1]

The pregnancy of the woman

Will you understand me if I say the Old Testament is a period of pregnancy? That pregnancy began in the third chapter of Genesis. There, as we have noted, we find the account of Satan enticing Adam and Eve into sin.

God had made Adam and Eve to live for his glory, as he had with Lucifer. And now it appeared that Satan had defeated God's purpose. Adam and Eve had failed to do that for which God had created them.

---

[1] Frederick S. Leahy, *The Victory of the Lamb*, The Banner of Truth Trust, Edinburgh, 2001, p.9.

But God would not allow Satan to have the victory. There in the Garden of Eden, God announced his plan to send the Messiah who would redeem God's people from their sin and cause them again to live for the glory of God. That promise was stated in these words that God spoke to Satan:

> And I will put enmity
> Between you and the woman,
> And between your seed and her Seed;
> He shall bruise your head,
> And you shall bruise his heel.
> (Gen. 3:15)

That promise struck terror into Satan's heart. It foretold the destruction of his kingdom by the Messiah. It declared that the Messiah would crush Satan's head. From the time Satan heard this promise, he sought to keep it from being fulfilled.

That promise also marked the beginning of the pregnancy of the woman of Revelation 12. From that time, the people of God began to look forward to the coming of the Messiah. They began, as it were, crying out in anguish and travail. The entire Old Testament period was, we might say, a time of labour for the people of God, in which they yearned for the Messiah finally to be delivered.

They brought their sacrifices to God, recognising as they did so that those sacrifices could not actually atone for sin. Only the Messiah could do that. As the people of God waited, they could see Satan's kingdom making advances, and they yearned for the Messiah, recognising that he alone could put an end to Satan and his kingdom.

The waiting and yearning finally ended when the Lord Jesus Christ was born in Bethlehem. The period of pregnancy was over and the people of God rejoiced in the birth of Christ. When Christ was born, all of God's people of the Old Testament could join with Isaiah the prophet in proclaiming:

14

Behold, this is our God;
We have waited for him,
and he will save us.
This is the LORD;
We have waited for him;
We will be glad and rejoice
in his salvation.

(Isa. 25:9)

Christmas is a time of rejoicing because it proves that God has fulfilled his promise. Because God has kept this promise, the greatest of all his promises, we can rest assured that he will also keep all the others. One of those promises is that he will grant forgiveness of sins to all those who come to him in true repentance and faith. Don't be among the multitudes that celebrate Christmas each year without having truly received the Christ of Christmas.

2.

The dragon seeking to devour the Child

Read: Revelation 12:1-6

We are rejoicing again this Christmas season in God's plan of redemption, and we are doing so on the basis of the opening verses of Revelation 12. There we find that we are part of a great drama that has been working its way out in all of human history. This drama consists of three major characters: a woman, a child and a dragon.

We have identified the child as Christ (v.5), the dragon as Satan (v.9) and the woman as the people of God in the Old Testament who were 'pregnant' with the promise God made to Adam and Eve. That promise was to send the Messiah, who would redeem them from their sin and crush Satan's kingdom (Gen. 3:15).

When Satan heard that promise, he realised that he must at all costs prevent the Messiah from coming. To use the terminology of Revelation 12, he 'stood before the woman who was ready to give birth, to devour her child'.

The whole Old Testament period was simultaneously, therefore, a time in which the people of God were yearning for God's promise to be fulfilled, and a time in which Satan was seeking to stop it from being fulfilled.

Satan is not equal to God, but he is a powerful foe. That is brought out very clearly in Revelation 12. We are told that he had 'seven heads and ten horns, and seven diadems on his heads' (v.3b). These are symbolic terms to reflect his power and dominion. The seven heads with the seven crowns depict his usurped dominion. The horn represents power, and the number ten represents completeness. The fact that Satan has ten horns, therefore, reflects the completeness of his power over the kingdoms of the earth. We should not miss another part of the description, that is, his 'fiery red' colour (v.3). This represents his murderous character.

When Satan heard God promise that the Messiah would come and crush his [Satan's] kingdom, he began to muster all his power and all his ingenuity to keep that promise from being fulfilled. He began seeking to 'devour' the child.

We have several instances in the Old Testament in which it appears that Satan would succeed, that the promise would be thwarted and the Messiah would never come.

Pharaoh's decree

One of these instances occurred when all the descendants of Jacob were forced by famine to move to Egypt. After Joseph died, a Pharaoh arose that subjected the Israelite people to oppressive slavery. At one point, Pharaoh ordered all newborn Israelite males to be killed (Exod. 1:15-22). The decree of Pharaoh might look to us as nothing more than a king employing a political strategy that was fairly common in those days. But behind Pharaoh's decision was the sinister hand of Satan. Satan knew that Israel had been designated by God as the nation from which the Messiah would come. If there was no nation of Israel, there could be no Messiah.

We know that this attempt to destroy Israel was thwarted; the Hebrew population continued to grow. We also know that Israel did not stay in bondage in Egypt. God delivered her in due time. Frederick Leahy summarises in this way: 'Thus God overruled the Satanic assault on Israel directed by Pharaoh...the Messianic line stood firm.'[2]

Athaliah's plot

Another of Satan's attempts to destroy the messianic promise is described in 2 Kings 11 and 2 Chronicles 22 and 23. These chapters describe a terribly dark and dismal time in the kingdom of Judah. The whole nation was plummeting into apostasy and

---

2 Frederick S. Leahy, *The Victory of the Lamb*, The Banner of Truth Trust, Edinburgh, 2001, p.30.

idolatry. Jehoram, king of Judah and son of the godly Jehoshaphat, had married the daughter of Ahab (2 Kings 8:16-18).

As soon as we hear the name 'Ahab', we think of Baal worship. Ahab was the king of Israel who brought Baal worship into his kingdom in an unprecedented and official way.

The fact that Jehoram had married the daughter of Ahab guaranteed that Judah would begin to walk the same dark path her sister kingdom Israel had been treading (2 Kings 8:18). This woman, the daughter of Ahab, saw her husband die and her son Ahaziah ascend the throne of Judah. When her son was assassinated, she saw her opportunity and seized the throne for herself (2 Kings 11:1). There was no doubt in her mind about the first order of business. She immediately set about to destroy 'all the royal heirs' (2 Kings 11:1).

We must remind ourselves at this point that the kingdom of Judah was ruled by the house of David. All the royal heirs were, therefore, descendants of David. Athaliah's plan therefore was to destroy all David's house so that he would have no more descendants.

What is so significant about this? Just that the house of David was the house from which the Messiah would spring. God clearly promised that the Messiah would be a descendant of David (2 Sam. 7:12-16). If the house of David was destroyed that promise could not be fulfilled.

Does this matter? Indeed it does. God's kingdom is one of truth, and if God's promise to make the Messiah a descendant of David had come to nothing, God's character and kingdom would have been hopelessly compromised.

Athaliah came very close to her goal. She succeeded in eliminating all the house of David except for one child, Joash, who was hidden away by a priest named Jehoiada and his wife Jehosheba (2 Kings 11:2). For six long years they hid the child, and when he was seven years old they succeeded in getting him crowned as king and in deposing the wicked Athaliah.

It is important for us to understand that the wickedness of

Athaliah was prompted by Satan himself, and her evil scheme to destroy the house of David was nothing less than Satan's scheme to thwart the promise of God. But his scheme failed. And the house of David survived.

Israel in exile

We can find yet another example by looking at a later time in the history of the kingdom of Judah. This kingdom continued to drift from God and his laws. The Lord sent prophet after prophet to warn the kings and the people of Judah that they must repent of their sins or experience devastating judgement.

The kings and the people spurned the message of the prophets, and God's judgement came upon them just as those prophets had promised. It arrived in the form of Babylon. This foreign nation invaded Judah and destroyed the city of Jerusalem and the beautiful temple of Solomon. The Babylonians also carried away most of the people back to Babylon as captives (2 Kings 25:1-21).

For seventy long years they stayed in Babylon. It must often have seemed to the faithful Jews that they would become completely absorbed in Babylon – that they would never get back to their land. It also seemed to them that the house of David would not survive and that the promise of the Messiah would be forfeited. Satan again seemed to be on the verge of succeeding in his attempt to overthrow the promise of God. But the house of David did indeed survive the captivity. The last chapter of 2 Kings refers to Jehoiachin being treated kindly in Babylon. What is the significance of this? Jehoiachin was a descendant of David (2 Kings 25:27-30)!

It should be noted that the instances we have described are only a few of the many attempts of Satan to overthrow the promise of the Messiah.

We rejoice that all of his attempts failed and the promise was fulfilled. The Messiah came as promised. Because he came we may receive forgiveness of our sins and eternal life by trusting in him alone as our Lord and Saviour.

19

3.
The dragon and the
first Christmas

Read: Matthew 2:1-18

Revelation 12 presents us with a woman, a child and a dragon. We have been able to identify the child as the Lord Jesus Christ, the dragon as Satan and the woman as the people of God who were pregnant with God's promise to send the Messiah.

When Satan heard God's promise that the Messiah would destroy his kingdom, he set himself to keep that promise from being fulfilled. Revelation 12:4 puts it in this way: 'the dragon stood before the woman who was ready to give birth, to devour her child'.

We have looked at some instances in the Old Testament when Satan strove mightily against the messianic promise, instances in which it seemed that he would succeed. But in each case he was defeated and the promise of God stayed on course.

Century gave way to century, and the people of God continued to look forward to the fulfilment of the promise. The Old Testament era ended and four hundred long years ensued in which God gave no new revelation. Almost certainly, many of the saints of God would have wondered whether the Messiah would ever come.

Then one grand day, God broke his silence. A priest, Zacharias, was burning incense in the temple when an angel appeared to announce that Zacharias' wife, Elizabeth, would bear a son who would be the forerunner of the Messiah. The Messiah was now at the door!

A while later the same angel, Gabriel, appeared to a Jewish maiden to make this announcement: 'behold, you will conceive in your womb and bring forth a Son, and shall call his name

Jesus. He will be great, and will be called the Son of the Highest; and the Lord God will give him the throne of his father David. And he will reign over the house of Jacob for ever, and of his kingdom there will be no end' (Luke 1:31-33).

An angel also appeared to Joseph, saying: 'Joseph, son of David, do not be afraid to take to you Mary your wife, for that which is conceived in her is of the Holy Spirit. And she will bring forth a son, and you shall call his name Jesus, for he will save his people from their sins' (Matt. 1:20-21).

A few months later Joseph and Mary took their journey to Bethlehem, and there, just as the prophet Micah had foretold (Micah 5:2), the Lord Jesus was born.

Do we understand the significance of this? We get so caught up with the angels, the shepherds, the star and the wise men, that we lose sight of this central truth – with all his devices, schemes and machinations, Satan had been unable to thwart the promise. But Satan was not ready to give up the battle. He had not been able to keep Jesus from being born, but he could now seek to have him killed. Satan had ready at hand an instrument for this purpose – Herod the king.

We have in Matthew 2 the account of how Satan used Herod to launch a cold-blooded scheme. Matthew begins his story with Herod receiving guests from the East. These men came to Herod with this question: 'Where is he who has been born King of the Jews? For we have seen his star in the East and have come to worship him' (Matt. 2:2). This word brought terror to Herod's heart. Intending to tolerate no rivals, the king sprang into action. He first gathered 'all the chief priests and scribes' to determine where this king had been born (v.4). He then called for the Magi so he could determine the time when this king had been born (v.7).

With place and time established, Herod employed:

A deceptive strategy
He sent the Magi to Bethlehem with these instructions: 'Go and search carefully for the young child, and when you have found

him, bring back word to me, that I may come and worship him also' (v.8). The Magi evidently accepted this instruction at face value and intended to comply with it. As they began their journey, the same star they had seen in the East appeared and led them to the Lord Jesus. Upon seeing him, they fell down in worship and presented their gifts (vv.9-11).

But they did not go back to Herod. Matthew says: 'Then, being divinely warned in a dream that they should not return to Herod, they departed for their own country another way' (v.12).

His deceptive strategy having failed, Herod resorted to:

A violent strategy

Matthew describes it in this way: 'Then Herod, when he saw that he was deceived by the wise men, was exceedingly angry; and he sent forth and put to death all the male children who were in Bethlehem and in all its districts, from two years old and under, according to the time which he had determined from the wise men' (v.16).

It should be clear to us that the wise men did not arrive in Bethlehem on the same night Jesus was born. Herod's decree indicates that Jesus was about two years old by the time the Magi arrived. But the point of focus for us is the cold, heartless nature of this man Herod. To protect his own throne he was willing to resort to unspeakable atrocities, sending his soldiers through Bethlehem and the surrounding area to tear baby boys away from their mothers and put them to death.

The tragedy of Herod's violence is compounded by this: Jesus posed no threat to him and his throne. Jesus did not come to be a political king. He came to set up a spiritual kingdom in the hearts of his people.

The violent strategy of Herod worked no better than his deceptive strategy. Matthew explains: 'an angel of the Lord appeared to Joseph in a dream, saying, "Arise, take the young child and his mother, flee to Egypt, and stay there until I bring you word; for Herod will seek the young child to destroy him" ' (v.13).

To say that Herod's plan failed is, of course, to say that Satan's plan failed, because it was Satan that prompted Herod to act as he did.

Lessons to learn

What are we to take away from all this? How are we to apply it to ourselves? I suggest the following:

1. Satan has not allowed all his defeats to stop him. He was not able to stop the Lord Jesus from coming, and not able to kill him after he came. But he is still the furious dragon described in Revelation 12. He still hates God and opposes his kingdom in every way he can. This means that he hates the people of God and does all he can to defeat them. The people of God are called, therefore, to resist him by taking up the whole armour of God (Eph. 6:10-20).

2. Satan is using the same strategies against the people of God today that he used in Matthew 2. He has his deceptive strategy in which he tries to seduce people away from the truth of God and the ways of God by using the smooth, pleasant words of false teachers. He has also his violent strategy, in which he incites persecution against the people of God.

3. God is greater than Satan. While Satan is a powerful and dreadful foe, he is not the equal of God. As the Lord had sufficient resources to defeat Satan's scheme – giving the wise men a dream and sending an angel to Joseph – so he has sufficient resources to continue defeating Satan.

4. All the promises of God are absolutely sure and indestructible. Satan could not thwart God's promise to send Christ, and he will not be able to defeat any of his other promises.

We must not leave this passage without pondering these words: 'But when Herod was dead' (v.19). Herod was not able to kill Jesus, but neither was he able to escape death himself. In God's time, death found him and took him.

Every unbeliever would do well to pay heed to this. It is possible to go through life filled with hatred for God and resisting God and his truth. But no amount of hatred and resistance will ever succeed against him. Every single one of us must finally meet the Lord. The only question is whether we will meet him as our welcoming Father or as our condemning Judge.

If we would meet him as the former, we must repent of our sins and trust completely in the redeeming work of the Christ of Christmas.

4.
Christ is born, Satan is defeated

Read: Revelation 12:5; Luke 2:1-7

We have been looking at God's marvellous plan of redemption through the lens of the opening verses of Revelation 12. These verses present the basis of a drama consisting of three major characters: a woman, a child and a dragon.

We have identified the child as the Lord Jesus Christ, the dragon as Satan, and the woman as the people of God who were yearning for the Messiah to come. We have also noted how Satan first tried to keep the promise of the Messiah from being fulfilled and, having failed, then attempted to destroy the Christ-child. He was, of course, defeated again.

In the days leading up to Christmas, we rejoice in our God and in his defeat of Satan. We may do so by looking again at Revelation 12 and at the opening verses of Luke 2. On the basis of these passages, we can make some glorious affirmations.

First, because God defeated all Satan's attempts to destroy the Messiah, we have:

A wonder to behold

We find that wonder in the word 'child.' The apostle John says: 'And she bore a male child' (Rev.12:5). We must not let this season pass without weighing the significance of this. The second person of the Trinity, the Lord God himself, took unto himself our humanity, and did so by stepping into human history as a baby. Nevertheless, he did not cease in any form or fashion to be God.

Christmas therefore presents us with this wonder – God as a baby! Joseph S. Cook captured something of this wonder in these words:

Gentle Mary laid her Child
Lowly in a manger;
There he lay, the undefiled,
To the world a stranger;
Such a Babe in such a place,
Can he be the Saviour?

That brings us to yet another Christmas affirmation – because God defeated Satan's attempts to destroy the Messiah we have:

A Saviour to receive

This is, of course, the key truth of Christmas. And it is the truth upon which the angels fastened the attention of the shepherds outside Bethlehem: 'For there is born to you this day in the city of David a Saviour, who is Christ the Lord' (Luke 2:11).

That word 'Saviour' tells us about him, but it also tells us about ourselves. It tells us that there is something from which we need saving. The Bible is very clear on this. The thing from which we need to be saved is the wrath of God. And the reason why we are under the wrath of God? It is all due to our sins. But the same God who has wrath against sin also has a love for sinners. Because of this love he sent his Son to save us from our sins (Matt. 1:21, John 3:16).

How did Jesus provide salvation? On the cross he received the wrath of God. There is, therefore, no wrath left for the believing sinner (2 Cor. 5:21; 1 Peter 2:24).

Think again about these words from Joseph Cook:

Such a Babe in such a place,
Can he be the Saviour?

The answer, thank God, is an emphatic and glorious Yes! That baby, lying there in the manger, came to this earth to be the Saviour. He came to Bethlehem so that he could go to Calvary, and there provide salvation.

26

It is no wonder that Luke closes his Christmas story with a comment on how the shepherds felt after they had seen the Saviour: 'Then the shepherds returned, glorifying and praising God for all the things that they had heard and seen, as it was told them' (Luke 2:20).

This compels me to ask: Is he your Saviour? It is not enough to know that Jesus came to be the Saviour. We must each receive him as our Saviour, as the only one who can deliver us from the penalty for our sins and enable us to stand acceptably before the holy God.

We now turn our attention again to Revelation 12:5 to add yet another Christmas affirmation. Because God defeated Satan's attempts to destroy the Messiah, we have:

A victor to admire

We can say this on the basis of these words: 'And she bore a male child...and her child was caught up to God and to his throne' (Rev. 12:5).

We have in these words both the beginning and the end of Jesus' time on earth, that is, his birth and his ascension.

Do we appreciate the significance of the ascension? In receiving Christ back into heaven, God the Father was expressing his delight with everything that the Lord Jesus did on this earth. God was completely satisfied with the life Jesus lived and with the death that he died. The ascension also shows the completeness of God's victory. As well as sending the Lord Jesus Christ into this world, God received him back into glory. All Satan's attempts to destroy God's plan of redemption completely failed. The Lord Jesus came to earth, did the work he was commissioned to do and then returned to heaven. Christ is the victor and Satan is the loser.

Revelation 12:5 contains yet another phrase which enables us to add a final affirmation. Because God has defeated Satan we have:

A ruler to whom we must submit

We base this affirmation on these words: 'And she bore a male child who was to rule all nations with a rod of iron' (Rev. 12:5). The word 'nations' simply means 'peoples'. The verse states therefore that the little baby in Bethlehem is eventually going to rule over all. This will constitute the fulfilment of Psalm 2:8-9, where God the Father says to the Son:

> Ask of me, and I will give you
> The nations for your inheritance,
> And the ends of the earth for your possession.
> You shall break them with a rod of iron,
> You shall dash them in pieces like a potter's vessel.

He is ruling now. After he had risen from the grave, he said to his disciples: 'All authority has been given to me in heaven and on earth' (Matt. 28:18). There is not so much as a single blade of grass that moves apart from his sovereign permission.

But Christ's rule is not universally acknowledged. He rules, but many deny his rule. They do not realise that the one whom they deny gives to them the very breath they need to make their denials. The Lord Jesus is now patiently enduring the wicked, but a day is coming in which his patience will come to an end. On that day, he will no longer allow them to deny his sovereign authority. He will crush all opposition and will require every knee to bow before him and every tongue to confess what has been true all along, namely, that he is indeed Lord of all (Phil. 2:9-11).

> *Thy foes in vain designs engage*
> *Against his throne, in vain they rage;*
> *Like rising waves with angry roar*
> *That dash and die upon the shore.*
> (Isaac Watts)

While the rule or government of Christ over all will bring

terror to those who oppose him, it will bring immeasurable comfort to those who love him. The government of Christ at the end of the world will cause them no terror, because they have lived under that government on this earth. They will have no trouble bowing before him then, because they have bowed before him here. Christ is only a terror to those who refuse his rule. Those who submit to it find that he is gracious and kind beyond measure.

The most urgent business in this life, therefore, is to bow before the Lord Jesus Christ, acknowledging that we are sinners and that he is our rightful Lord. Our choice is to bow now and receive his salvation, or bow later and receive his judgement.

> *Ye sinners, seek His grace,*
> *Whose wrath ye cannot bear;*
> *Fly to the shelter of His cross,*
> *And find salvation there!*
>
> (Philip Doddridge)

Section 2

Why do we need Christmas?

5.
The cup is in the bag

Read: Genesis 44

The further modern societies drift from Christianity, the less Christians can take for granted. When Christmas rolls around we cannot, for instance, take for granted that those around us will have adequate understanding of its meaning. Even believers themselves seem less sure-footed in explaining the meaning of Christmas than former generations.

Christmas represents more for Christians, therefore, than a cause to celebrate. It is also a challenge for us to clearly explain its meaning to others.

I am taking up the challenge of this Christmas by posing the question: Why do we need Christmas? My answers to that question seem to be somewhat bizarre. They are as follows:

The cup is in the bag
The harvest is in the field
The little foxes are in the vineyard
The boat is being tossed by the waves.

Some will be inclined to view these answers with suspicion, perhaps dismissing them as the attempt of an unwitty man to be clever. I plead guilty to devising such answers in order to excite and secure interest. But I also believe that all my readers will ultimately find that each answer takes us to the very heart of Christmas.

My first answer is drawn from the passage before us. To understand it, we must first recall some of the major details in the life of Joseph:

● he was hated by his brothers and sold into slavery in Egypt

- in Egypt he interpreted a dream for Pharaoh, a dream that indicated that seven years of severe famine would arise for Egypt and the surrounding nations
- he was rewarded for interpreting this dream by being made second to Pharaoh in authority, and he was specifically charged with the task of preparing Egypt for the years of famine
- his brothers came from the land of Canaan to seek food, which Joseph provided without, however, revealing his identity to them.

With these details in mind, we are ready to look at the passage before us. When Joseph had the sacks of the men filled with grain, he instructed his steward to put his own cup in the sack of his younger brother Benjamin. He did this to test his older brothers, to see if they would do to Benjamin what, years earlier, they had done to Joseph himself. In other words, he did it to see if they would be willing to leave Benjamin in slavery in Egypt, as they had done to him, or if they would stand with their younger brother. The story ends happily. The older brothers had indeed changed. They went back with Benjamin to Joseph, and their one brother, Judah, wholeheartedly interceded for Benjamin (44:18-34). Joseph responded by revealing his identity and was reconciled to his brothers (45:1).

But let's come back to this business of Joseph's cup. He had it placed in Benjamin's sack, and then sent his steward after his brothers to take as slave the man in whose sack the cup was found (v.10). Joseph's brothers steadfastly insisted that no one had stolen the cup, but it was found in Benjamin's sack.

What does all this have to do with us and with this Christmas season?

A gripping picture of ourselves and our sinful condition

Let us never forget that Christmas was designed to deal with our sin. The angel said to another Joseph, the one who would take Jesus' mother to be his wife: 'And she will bring forth a son, and you shall call his name Jesus, for he will save his people from their sins' (Matt. 1:21).

Modern ears do not like to hear this. People become indignant when they are confronted with the reality of their sin. Some, when they hear a preacher charge them with sin, respond by saying: 'Who does that preacher think he is? What right does he have to call me a sinner?' My answer to that charge is that the cup is in the bag.

In other words, we can deny the reality of our sin as much as we want, but there is indisputable proof of it, and all the denials in the world will not do away with it. Joseph's brothers hotly denied having his cup, but the cup was there.

What is sin? It is simply the failure to conform to the laws of God. What are the laws of God? We can find them in the Ten Commandments. Here are a few of them:

- we are not to have any other gods (Exod. 20:3). Have you placed anything else before God? Have you given anything else the love and devotion that belong to him alone? The cup is in the bag!
- we are not to take God's name in vain (Exod. 20:7). Have you used God's name loosely and carelessly? The cup is in the bag!
- we are to honour our parents (Exod. 20:12). We are to obey them in our young years and respect them in our older years. Have you done these things? Have you always obeyed? Have you always spoken respectfully of them? The cup is in the bag!
- we are not to lie (Exod. 20:16). Have we always spoken the truth? The cup is in the bag!

These are only four of the Ten Commandments. But it does not matter which of the ten we look at, the answer is the same. We have failed to obey them. We have broken God's laws. We stand guilty and condemned before him. Just as Joseph had evidence against his brothers, so God has evidence against us. We stand before God without any plea and without any bargaining power.

A picture of God's willingness to forgive freely and completely

When the cup was found in Benjamin's sack, all the men were grief-stricken. Judah responded to Joseph in this way: 'What shall we say to my lord? What shall we speak? Or how shall we clear ourselves? God has found out the iniquity of your servants; here we are, my lord's slaves, both we and he also with whom the cup was found' (v.16).

We have in the words of Judah an example of genuine repentance. Judah treated Joseph with the utmost respect. He admitted that he and his brothers had no bargaining power. He submitted completely to the one who had authority over him and the one against whom he and his brothers had sinned.

If you and I nurse any hopes of being cleared before God, we must follow Judah's example. We must stop harbouring evil thoughts about God and speaking against him and his ways. We must admit that we are guilty and have no bargaining power. And we must cast ourselves entirely upon the mercy of the one who has authority over us.

This is genuine repentance. When we come to this kind of repentance, we find free and complete forgiveness from God, even as Joseph's brother found forgiveness from him.

How can God forgive guilty sinners? Does he simply ignore their sins? No, he cannot do that. His holy nature requires him to judge sin. If God did not judge sin, he would be guilty of sin himself and would cease to be God.

God can and does grant forgiveness for our sins on the basis of Christmas. Christmas means God sent his Son. And Jesus came to do two things. First, he lived a perfect life. He perfectly complied with all of God's laws. You can search and search, and you will never find a cup in the sack of Jesus' life. You will rather be compelled to join Pontius Pilate in saying: *'I find no fault in him at all'* (John 18:38). Secondly, the Lord

Jesus Christ went to a Roman cross to die a special kind of death. There he received the wrath of God in the place of sinners. Since the wrath of God against my sins was poured out on Jesus, there is no wrath left for me.

The gospel of Christ is simply this: by his life Jesus provided the righteousness I do not have, and by his death he took the penalty I deserve. When I stop defending myself before God and sincerely come to him freely admitting that his cup is in the sack of my life, God forgives on the basis of what Jesus Christ did for sinners.

We need Christmas, because we are sinners who need a Saviour. By means of Christmas God provided that Saviour. At Christmas we rejoice in the truth of these words:

> 'For there is born to you this day in the city of David a Saviour, who is Christ the Lord.'

> (Luke 2:11)

6.
The harvest is in the field

Read: Matthew 9:35-38

Confusion and wrong thinking about Christmas seem to grow with each passing year. It is increasingly necessary, therefore, for Christians to think deeply about the meaning of Christmas and to explain it clearly to others.

To help us along this path, I am posing the question: Why do we need Christmas? I could also put it in this way: Why is Christmas important?

My first answer to that question was, 'The cup is in the bag.' By that I simply meant that we need Christmas because the cup of sin has been found in the sack of our lives. We stand guilty before God, and we have absolutely no excuse and no bargaining power. Each of our lives provides indisputable evidence that God's charge against us – that we are sinners – is true. Christmas means that God sent his Son to provide forgiveness for our sins. We need Christmas because we need forgiveness.

That first answer was directed to all without exception. We are all sinners and we need to be saved. This second answer is directed towards Christians. We who believe in Christ need Christmas because 'The harvest is in the field'.

Like it or not, all Christians are in the harvesting business. This world is a gigantic field, and heaven is a gigantic barn (Matt. 3:12). The Lord has called us, his followers, to go out into the field and gather people for heaven. In other words, all Christians are called to do mission work or to be missionaries. Christmas is essentially missions. It celebrates the mission work of God himself. God came into the field of this world through his Son for the express purpose of seeking and saving the lost (Luke 19:10).

When this mission was complete and the Lord Jesus Christ was

38

ready to return to the Father in heaven, he, the Lord Jesus, said to his disciples: 'you shall be witnesses to me' (Acts 1:8). This was nothing new. A few days earlier Jesus had said to them: 'As the Father has sent me, I also send you' (John 20:21). Although God's people have been clearly called to be involved in the work of harvesting souls, the truth is we are constantly inclined to neglect this vital work. We have become religious consumers, more concerned that the church should meet our needs than that we should meet the needs of others. Sadly enough, many Christians give the impression that the fields are empty, and all that remains is for us to sit idly in the house.

We need Christmas because it reminds us that this is not the case. It reminds us of God's missionary activity on our behalf and the need for us to be missionary-minded as well.

The verses of our text give us insight into this matter of harvesting for the Lord. They reveal a couple of essential truths about spiritual harvesting.

Harvesting requires us to understand spiritual realities

Verse 36 tells us that Jesus 'saw the multitudes' and 'was moved with compassion for them, because they were weary and scattered, like sheep having no shepherd'. In other words, Jesus saw beyond the physical realities to the spiritual. If you and I had been there, we would have been able to see the physical side easily. We would have been able to see the milling multitude and some of the signs of their various afflictions. But Jesus saw the spiritual side.

Are we seeing the spiritual side today? As we journey along life's pathway, we constantly encounter people. Do we consistently think of them in spiritual terms? Do we only see people living in this temporal realm, or do we remember that everyone we meet is an eternity-bound person? Do we remember that eternity consists of two parts – destruction and bliss – and that only those who know Christ will enter the bliss?

A perfect example of this is found in the fourth chapter of John's gospel. There we find the Lord Jesus sharing the good

39

news of salvation with a woman from Samaria. When the disciples returned from the nearby town with food, they said to him: 'Rabbi, eat.' Jesus responded: 'I have food to eat of which you do not know.' The disciples, mystified by this, said: 'Has anyone brought him anything to eat?'

They were thinking exclusively in terms of the physical, but Jesus was thinking of the spiritual. He said: 'My food is to do the will of him who sent me, and to finish his work.'

Jesus then pointed them to the reality of a vast spiritual harvest: 'Do you not say, "There are still four months and then comes the harvest?" Behold, I say to you, lift up your eyes and look at the fields, for they are already white for harvest!' (John 4:31-35). What was Jesus saying? If anyone had asked the disciples about the harvest, they, thinking about the physical harvest, would have said: 'That's four months away.'

Jesus wanted them to understand that there was even then a far greater harvest, a harvest of souls that was already ripe and waiting only for the harvesters. He was calling them to look beyond the physical to the spiritual. We will never harvest until we understand spiritual realities.

Harvesting requires us to act

Jesus could not be content with merely looking upon the multitude. He could not be content with merely feeling compassion for them. What he saw and what he felt compelled him to take action. Mark's Gospel makes this clear. It says of Jesus: 'So he began to teach them many things' (Mark 6:34). Understanding led to compassion, and compassion led to action. Compassion for souls will lead us to action as well.

What actions constitute spiritual harvesting? In other words, what actions can we take that will be effective in reaping souls for Christ?

The Lord Jesus specified one action. He said to his disciples: 'The harvest truly is plentiful, but the labourers are few. Therefore ask [pray] the Lord of the harvest to send out labourers into his harvest' (Matt. 9:37-38).

Praying is, then, an essential part of harvesting. For whom are we to pray? Pray for all those who proclaim the gospel and pray for all those who hear it and need to hear it!

Another way in which we can engage in harvesting is through providing financial support for gospel enterprises. In the midst of a financial appeal to the Corinthians, the apostle Paul writes: 'He who sows sparingly will also reap sparingly, and he who sows bountifully will also reap bountifully. So let each one give as he purposes in his heart, not grudgingly or of necessity; for God loves a cheerful giver' (2 Cor. 9:6-7). It is shameful that so many Christians these days spend so much money on their entertainment and comfort, and so little on the work of the Lord. May God help each of us to give more generously than we have in the past!

Another thing we can do to engage in spiritual harvesting is promote the well-being of our church and her ministry. Those who engage in tearing the church down are essentially poking holes in the bottom of the lifeboat! Part of promoting the well-being of the church is the manner in which we approach worship. As we gather for worship, we should remember that there is a sense in which we are on display. Unbelievers in our midst are drawing conclusions about Christianity on the basis of what they observe in us. If we appear to be bored or distracted, they may very well conclude that there is nothing to it.

There is, of course, another way in which we can harvest for Christ, and that is by sharing the gospel message with unbelieving family members and friends.

How thankful we should be that the Christmas season has rolled around again! We sorely need it! We need it because we so easily come out of the harvest field. Christmas reminds us that our harvesting God has called us to join him in the fields, and the fields are white.

41

7.
The little foxes are
in the vineyard

Read: Song of Solomon 2:15

Why do we need Christmas? To this question we have provided two answers. The first was, 'The cup is in the bag'. In other words, we need Christmas because God charges us with sin, and we cannot deny this charge. God, so to speak, has the goods on us. How thankful we should be that he could not be content with charging us with sin. He also provided a way for our sins to be forgiven. That way is his Son, Jesus Christ. And, of course, that is what we celebrate at Christmas: the coming of God's Son to this earth to provide eternal salvation for those who believe.

The second answer to this important question was, 'The harvest is in the field'. Christmas celebrates God coming into his harvest field to gather souls for heaven. Each year it reminds us that he has appointed his people to do the same.

Now we look at a third answer, namely, 'The little foxes are in the vineyard.'

We draw this answer from the Song of Solomon. This book is a love story. It tells us about the king of Israel, Solomon, falling in love with a country girl. This young woman had brothers who evidently treated her harshly. They made her work so hard in the family vineyard that she virtually had no time to care for her appearance (1: 5-6). Our text presents us with yet another responsibility assigned to this young woman by her brothers:

> Catch us the foxes,
> The little foxes that spoil the vines,
> For our vines have tender grapes.

The vineyard was evidently being severely damaged by little foxes. These playful young foxes were probable chewing on the vines and ripping off the grapes, and the brothers of the young woman wanted her to put a stop to it by setting traps for them.

Those who are familiar with the history of biblical interpretation know that another level of understanding of the Song of Solomon has been widely embraced down through the centuries. This level sees the Song as a picture of Christ's love for his people and their love for him. This approach views the various details of the Song in a spiritual way, looking for spiritual lessons and applications from each aspect of the Song.

With that approach in mind, we find the words of our text speaking very powerfully to us about a terrible tendency in our own lives – the tendency to allow small, trivial things to overrun and destroy what is truly important.

Let's explore this tendency:

Our lives as vines

It is no great stretch of imagination for us to think in these terms. The Bible often uses the imagery of a vine to convey the nature of our lives.

This is rich imagery. It tells us that we are not here by accident. God has planted us. And he has planted us for a very special and important purpose, namely, to bear fruit for him. No one plants a vineyard without the intention of enjoying the fruit of that vineyard, and God has planted us with the intention of enjoying fruit from our lives.

How do we bear fruit for God? How can we live in such a way as to bring pleasure to him? What does God want from our lives? The Lord Jesus Christ himself answers these questions in these words:

> The first of all the commandments is: 'Hear, O Israel,the Lord our God, the Lord is one. And you shall love the Lord your God with all your heart, with all your soul, with all your mind, and with all your strength.' This is the first commandment. And the second, like it, is this: 'You shall love your neighbour as yourself.' There is no other commandment greater than these.
>
> (Mark 12:29-31)

43

How are we to express such love for God? We must obey his commandments. We must live for his glory. We must worship him seriously and sincerely.

We know these things. We know that we are to live for God. We know we are to give him first place in our lives. We know he is worthy of our love. We know that we are to be faithful to his house. We know that we are to support his work with our time, our energy, and, yes, our money. We also know how we struggle to live as we ought. Someone has rightly observed that while the Christian life is glorious, it is not easy. It is no accident that the cross is the symbol of Christianity. The cross represents dying to self and living to God. It represents hardship, pain and anguish. And we experience all of these things as we seek to live in the way God has commanded.

Why is the Christian life so hard for us? Why do we struggle so much to live as we ought? Much of the answer lies in the second consideration placed before us by our text, namely:

The little foxes

The family vineyard for which the young woman in the Song was responsible was not being overrun and destroyed by huge, wild beasts. It was being devastated by little foxes.

Does this not speak very forcefully of the situation in our own lives? Does it not remind us that we so often let trivial things – little foxes – eat up and destroy those things that are truly important?

Which of the little foxes is working havoc in the vineyard of your life? Which ones are keeping you from giving to God what you should? Sheer 'busy-ness' with pleasures and responsibilities is a very active little fox that wrecks the vineyard of service for many. Anger and resentment towards someone is a little fox that keeps many from serving the Lord. Unhappiness with some aspect of the church's ministry is a little fox for some. Disappointment with God over the circumstances of life constitutes a little fox that keeps still others from serving as they should. Each one of us can probably think of our own little fox without any difficulty. Because these little foxes abound, we should be grateful that the Christmas season has rolled around again. It reminds us of what truly counts.

Think about it: the eternal God took unto himself our humanity in which he did everything necessary for our sins to be removed so that we might share his eternal glory when this life is over.

Think about what was his before he came. He was the Lord of heaven. He was in perfect fellowship with God the Father and God the Holy Spirit. He was the recipient of the praises of all the angels.

Think about what was his after he came. He came to this earth, not to dwell among the richest of men, but rather among the poorest of them.

His life would have been difficult enough had it been only a life of deprivation. It was also a life of opposition, as he endured tremendous hostility from the religious leaders.

His life, of course, led him to the cross, where he died a death that was totally unlike any death before or since. There on the cross he received the wrath of God in the place of sinners. There he was forsaken of God so that those sinners would never have to be forsaken.

This Christ arose from the grave on the third day and ascended to the Father in heaven. He is in heaven today as the forerunner of his people (Heb. 6:20). His presence there is the guarantee that his people will follow him and will share his glory. This will take place when he returns to take his people home. On that glad day, the dead in Christ will be raised from their graves, and living believers will be caught up together to meet them in the air (1 Thess. 4:13-18). The day of his coming will finally issue in new heavens and a new earth, where there will be no pain, no sorrow, no crying and no more death (Rev. 21:4).

This is all involved in our celebration of Christmas, and this is the God who calls us to serve him during our time on this earth. With a God like this and a future like this, how can we let little things get in our way? When we finally come into his presence, how very ashamed we will be if we had let the little foxes spoil the vineyard of our service!

Let us use this Christmas season to get rid of those foxes and to be renewed in our determination to count for him.

8.
The boat is being tossed
by the waves

Read: Matthew 14:22-33

If I were to ask you to compile a list of Scriptures with a Christmas theme, you would not include the one before us. It does not seem to have any connection with Christmas at all.

I suggest, however, that this passage can indeed lead us to Christmas and tell us why we so desperately need it.

The details of the story

The account begins with strong and emphatic language. It tells us that Jesus 'made' his disciples get into a boat to cross over to Capernaum. John's Gospel gives us more details. It tells us that after Jesus miraculously fed five thousand people, there was a strong desire among the people to make Jesus their earthly king. This, of course, was not the purpose for which he came. To keep his disciples from being swept along by this tidal wave of emotion, Jesus 'made' (Mark 6:45) them get into the boat to cross the lake while he stayed behind to pray (John 6:15-16; see also Mark 6:45-46).

The disciples had not rowed far when they encountered a ferocious storm. Matthew tells us the wind was 'contrary' (v.24). John says 'a great wind was blowing' (John 6:18).

The storm itself was an awesome thing, but the disciples were about to see some things that were even more awesome and eye-popping. First, Jesus walked on the water to where they were (v.25). Secondly, he enabled Simon Peter to do the same for a while and then rescued him when he began to sink (vv.28-31). Finally, the storm stopped abruptly as soon as Jesus stepped into the boat (v.32). We are not surprised to read, then, that 'those who were in the boat came and worshipped him, saying, "Truly you are the Son of God"' (v.33).

What these men saw caused them to realise afresh and anew that they were not in the presence of a mere man. The one with whom they had been associating was nothing less than God in human flesh. We might say God had been set before them in an unforgettable way. It is at this point that this passage takes on:

The glow of Christmas

The purpose of Christmas is to set God before us. We need Christmas because we need to have God set before us. Christmas sets God before us. On the night that the Lord Jesus was born, God set himself before the shepherds in a marvellous and unmistakable way. Luke says: 'an angel of the Lord stood before them, and the glory of the Lord shone around them' (Luke 2:9). And the angel delivered this message to the shepherds: 'there is born to you this day in the city of David a Saviour, who is Christ the Lord' (Luke 2:11).

Luke further writes: 'And suddenly there was with the angel a multitude of the heavenly host praising God and saying: "Glory to God in the highest, and on earth peace, good will towards men!"' (Luke 2:13-14). There was no doubt in the minds of the shepherds that God had set himself before them. They said: 'Let us now go to Bethlehem and see this thing that has come to pass, which the Lord has made known to us' (Luke 2:15).

That was, of course, both the beginning of Jesus' time on earth, and the beginning of God setting himself before people in an unprecedented way. Consider the following episodes from his life and ministry:

● After his disciples had fished all night without success, the Lord Jesus caused them to catch so many fish that their two boats began to sink. And realising that God had been set before them, Simon Peter cried out: 'Depart from me, for I am a sinful man, O Lord!' (Luke 5:8).

- Jesus caused a deaf and mute man to hear and speak, and all who heard about it 'were astonished beyond measure, saying, "He has done all things well. He makes both the deaf to hear and the mute to speak"' (Mark 7:37). God had been set before them!
- Jesus was transfigured, that is, took on a heavenly appearance before Peter, James and John (Mark 9:2-13), and those men realised that God had been set before them.
- Jesus raised Lazarus from the grave four days after he died (John 11:17-44). No one there even tried to deny that God had been set before them.
- When Jesus was crucified, the sun hid its face and deep darkness enveloped the land. When Jesus died, the Roman centurion realised God had been set before him, and he cried out: 'Truly this was the Son of God!' (Matt. 27:54).
- When the risen Christ appeared before Thomas, the doubting disciple realised that God had been set before him, and he exclaimed: 'My Lord and my God!' (John 20:28).

The life of Jesus set God before the disciples so powerfully and consistently that the apostle John was compelled to write: 'And the Word became flesh and dwelt among us, and we beheld his glory, the glory as of the only begotten of the Father, full of grace and truth' (John 1:14).

What does all this have to do with us? The God who set himself before people so magnificently at the first Christmas and in the life and ministry of the Lord Jesus still sets himself before people today. While he does this all the time and in many ways, there is a sense in which the Christmas season reminds us more forcefully of God being set before us.

The storms of life

It could very well be that the boat of your life is being rocked today by a howling storm. I am so glad to be able to say to you that the Christmas message sets before you the sovereign, almighty God who is more than sufficient for your situation.

It may be that the storm clouds of death are gathering over your head. Christmas reminds you that the eternal God came into human history to prepare us for eternity. The only way to face death is to take hold of the eternal life that God has provided in his Son. Nothing removes the sting of death so much as knowing that this life is not all that there is. It is in reality only a prelude to glory for all those who believe in Christ.

Perhaps the boat of your life is being rocked by circumstances that are so difficult and burdens that are so crushing that you don't know where to turn. The Christmas message reminds you that God has stepped into human history to be with his people. One of the names given to Jesus is 'Immanuel', which means 'God with us' (Matt. 1:23).

Perhaps the boat of your life is being tossed by personal sin and by guilt. The Christmas message reminds us that God has been set before us, and this God forgives his people their sins and restores them to usefulness.

It could be that the boat of your life is caught in the storm of doubt. You once believed the Word of God, but now you are not sure. Look again at Christmas. How do you explain it? It can be explained only in these terms: God is real, and he demonstrated his reality by setting himself before us in Christ.

Nothing is more important for individual Christians and for churches today than using the eyes of faith to see the God who has set himself before us. May he be pleased this Christmas to remind us that he is real, that his power is great and his promises are true. May he be pleased to cause us to look upon the Christ of Christmas, and say from our hearts: 'Truly you are the Son of God' (Matt. 14:33).

Section 3

Having a better Christmas

9.
A better representative

Read: Romans 5:15-19; Corinthians 15:45,47

Each Christmas seems to bring with it the desire to make it better than the previous Christmas. The quest for 'the best Christmas ever' never ends.

A popular song some years ago used the phrase 'looking for love in all the wrong places'.

Perhaps the reason we continue the quest for the best Christmas ever is that we are looking in the wrong places. To experience Christmas at its best, we must not look so much to Christmas as to Christ; not so much to the Christmas tree as to Calvary's tree; not so much to Christmas presents as to Christ's presence; not so much to food and fun as to faith in Christ and fellowship with him.

To help us along the way, I am proposing that we think about the Lord Jesus Christ as our better representative, better Saviour, better kinsman and better king. The best Christmas resides in seeing the best person who ever lived. A better Christmas is found through the better Christ!

We begin by looking at him as our better representative. To be more precise, I am referring to Christ in his capacity as a representative head.

A representative head of humanity means one whose actions counted for others, specifically for all those whom he was sent to represent. There have only been two representative heads over humanity, and there will never be another. The first was Adam. The second and last was Jesus. Part of what we are celebrating at Christmas is the coming of Jesus to be another Adam – and a far better one!

In what ways was Jesus superior to the first Adam?

53

The first Adam was a created being: the Lord Jesus Christ was not

The first man at one point was non-existent. He had no being at all. The second man was and is the eternal God. There never was a time when he did not exist. The first man was of the earth. The second man did not come up from the earth. He came down from heaven. He was 'the Lord from heaven' (1 Cor. 15:47).

The fact that Jesus was born as a baby to Mary does not mean that he was a mere man. We are dealing here with the very heart of the Christmas message. The second person of the Trinity, who was fully God, stepped into human history as a mortal man. In doing so, he did not cease to be God, because God cannot cease to be God. Rather, he added our humanity to his deity so that he is, at one and the same time, fully God and fully man without any contradiction or confusion between the two.

At Christmas we celebrate the coming of the eternal God among us as a man. We celebrate the truth of John's glorious statement: 'And the Word became flesh and dwelt among us, and we beheld his glory, the glory as of the only begotten of the Father, full of grace and truth' (John 1:14). We celebrate the glorious truth of Paul's simple statement: 'God was in Christ' (2 Cor. 5:19).

The first Adam disobeyed God: the Lord Jesus Christ perfectly obeyed

The first Adam was given one command to obey. He was not to eat the fruit of the tree of knowledge of good and evil. Adam failed to keep this one command. Even though he was placed in a perfect environment, he failed. He failed because he listened to Satan.

The Lord Jesus came to do what Adam failed to do. He came to obey God. But how different things were when Jesus stepped into the arena! While Adam sinned in a perfect world, Jesus came into a very imperfect world. But even in the face of every conceivable disadvantage, Jesus did not fail. He obeyed the law of God perfectly. He was far better than Adam in obedience!

Adam's sins made all his descendants sinners: Jesus' obedience makes his people righteous

This brings us to the very heart of the role of the representative head. As our representative head, Adam's sin counted for all of us. It was imputed to us. There is a sense in which we were all present in him and sinned with him. And because we share in Adam's sin, we share in his condemnation. We are by virtue of our sins under the wrath of God. Here is the great, throbbing question of the ages: how can sinners ever have the sentence of God's wrath removed and stand guiltless before him?

The answer lies in Jesus. He, and he alone, is the one who can lift the sentence of condemnation from us. He, and he alone, can qualify us to stand acceptably in the presence of God. Jesus does this by virtue of his perfect life and his substitutionary death.

Do we understand that God demands one hundred per cent perfection of us before he will allow us into heaven? We do not have that perfection, but Jesus does. He was righteous in every respect. And if we will come to God with true repentance for our sins, God will count the righteousness of Jesus as though it were ours. It is perfect righteousness, and we can stand before God in it without fear.

While we do not have perfection, we certainly do have sin, and that sin is the reason we stand under God's condemnation. The good news of the Bible is that Jesus not only came to provide us with the righteousness we need, but also to pay the penalty for the sins we have committed. We can never stand in God's presence until our sins are removed. God cannot ignore sin. His nature requires that he judge sin, and the judgment he has pronounced is eternal separation from himself and from all that is good and holy.

That penalty has to be paid. We either have to pay it ourselves or someone has to pay it for us. And the only one who can pay it for us is the Lord Jesus, because he is the only one who has no sins of his own for which to pay. Jesus paid this penalty on the cross. There he received an eternity's worth of separation from God for all who believe. God only requires that the penalty of eternal wrath be paid once, and if Jesus paid it in the stead of sinners, there is no penalty left for those sinners to pay.

Jesus, therefore, as the Second Adam, did everything that was necessary for Adam's sin to be reversed. God tells us that if we will stop excusing our sin, sincerely repent of it and cast ourselves completely on what Jesus has done, the perfect righteousness he provided with this life will be counted as though it were ours, and the penalty he paid on the cross will be counted as though it were ours.

With our sins paid for and the perfect righteousness of Christ covering us, we don't have to tremble before God's demands but can go happily to heaven. Those who receive what Christ did for sinners have the tyranny of sin and death broken in their lives. Spiritual death is replaced with spiritual life. The sentence of eternal death is removed, and the gift of eternal life is bestowed. And the sting of physical death is pulled, so that it becomes nothing more than the entrance into eternal glory.

And those who receive what Christ did in his life and death find themselves joyously singing with the hymn writer:

> *O loving wisdom of our God!*
> *When all was sin and shame,*
> *A second Adam to the fight*
> *And to the rescue came.*
>
> *O wisest love! That flesh and blood,*
> *Which did in Adam fail,*
> *Should strive afresh against the foe,*
> *Should strive and should prevail.*
>
> (John Henry Newman)

Christmas celebrates Jesus in this capacity of the Second Adam. This was the plan of God for saving sinners, and Christmas is the fulfilment of that plan. Have you received this plan? Have you cast yourself in repentance and faith on the work of Jesus as the Second Adam?

Jesus is not only the Second Adam: he is also the last Adam. That means there will never be another representative head of the human race. Each and every one of us belongs either to the first Adam or to the Second Adam. If we belong to the first, we will perish. If we belong to the Second, we will live.

10.

A better Saviour

Read: Genesis 41:53-57

We must be clear on this: there is only one true Saviour in the ultimate sense of that term.

There is only one Saviour from sin and eternal wrath, and that is Jesus. But there have been other saviours throughout history. Noah saved his family from the flood. Moses saved the people of Israel from bondage in Egypt. David saved his people from bondage to the Philistines. Joseph was a saviour. The above verses tell us that he saved people from starvation in a famine-ravaged time

We know Joseph's story. One of Jacob's twelve sons, he was despised and hated by his brothers. What was the reason for this hatred? Joseph transparently loved God and was given special revelations by God. It was as true then as it is now. Unredeemed people do not discern the things of God (1 Cor. 2:14). The dislike these men felt for their brother continued to build until it reached a crescendo. They seized him and sold him to Midianite traders who were on their way to Egypt. There he was sold as a slave to Potiphar. And there he encountered more trouble. Unhappy that he rebuffed her romantic advances, Potiphar's wife falsely accused him. But when things looked to be utterly bleak and beyond repair, God stepped in. There in his prison, Joseph developed a reputation for being able to interpret dreams, and this ability finally landed him before Pharaoh, who needed to have a couple of dreams interpreted.

The first consisted of seven extremely well-fed cows being eaten by seven thin, gaunt cows. The second featured seven plump heads of grain being replaced by seven thin heads. Joseph was equal to the occasion. The two dreams were one and the same. The fat cows and fat heads of grain represented seven years of unprecedented prosperity. And the gaunt cows and thin

58

heads of grain represented seven years of extreme, harsh famine. Egypt and the rest of that world were to experience seven years of booming prosperity, which would be followed by seven years of grinding famine and poverty.

Pharaoh immediately recognised that Joseph had accurately interpreted the dreams. As a reward he elevated him to a position of authority that made him second only to Pharaoh himself. Joseph was given the special assignment of preparing Egypt for the seven years of famine. He did well. All through the years of prosperity, he put grain in reserve for the years of famine. When the years of abundance were over, the storehouses of Egypt were full to the brim.

Then the famine began – horrible, devastating famine in Egypt and the surrounding countries. But Joseph was ready. Moses writes: 'The famine was over all the face of the earth, and Joseph opened all the storehouses and sold to the Egyptians. And the famine became severe in the land of Egypt. So all countries came to Joseph in Egypt to buy grain, because the famine was so severe in all lands' (vv.56-57). So Joseph was a saviour. He saved the lives of all the peoples who came to him during the years of famine – including those of his own brothers!

What does this have to do with us? We have come, through the goodness of God, to another Christmas season. And, as we all know, Christmas celebrates the birth of Jesus, who came to be our Saviour.

Centuries after Joseph of Egypt, another Joseph came along – the one who was engaged to a young woman named Mary. This Joseph was shocked to learn that she was already with child. How could this be? An angel appeared to him with this word of explanation: 'Joseph, son of David, do not be afraid to take to you Mary your wife, for that which is conceived in her is of the Holy Spirit. And she will bring forth a son, and you shall call his name Jesus, for he will save his people from their sins' (Matt. 1:20-21).

Jesus came to this world for the express purpose of being a Saviour. And all the saviours who preceded him pale in comparison. The Joseph of Genesis was one of the greatest saviours in history, but he cannot begin to compare with Jesus. Let's notice how superior Jesus' Saviourhood is to that of Joseph.

Joseph opened a temporal storehouse to meet a temporal need: the Lord Jesus opens a spiritual storehouse to meet a spiritual need

The people of Joseph's time were perishing physically, and his storehouse was the means by which he saved them. But there is a far worse kind of perishing than physical perishing! That is, spiritual perishing. It is that condition in which we are separated from God by virtue of our sins, that condition which will ultimately issue in eternal death. How foolish, then, are those who live exclusively for the things of life as if physical perishing were the only danger!

But there is good news for all who are spiritually perishing and all who are in danger of perishing eternally. God has a storehouse full of forgiveness for our sins! He has a storehouse of salvation!

Joseph had authority to open the storehouse of Egypt: Jesus opens the storehouse of salvation on the basis of far greater authority

The authority by which Joseph operated was Pharaoh's. The authority by which Jesus operated was God's. It was God who appointed him as the Saviour of sinners before the world began. It was God who laid the work of salvation before him, some of which we will note shortly. It was God who sent him. Let us, then, forever rid ourselves of the notion that God the Father is stern and reluctant to save, and that Jesus had to persuade him. God the Father, God the Son and God the Holy Spirit have always been in complete agreement on the issue of salvation.

But let us make sure that we understand that it is to Jesus alone that God has granted authority to open the storehouse of salvation. No one else can do so. Jesus himself said: 'All authority has been given to me in heaven and on earth'

(Matt. 28:18). And the apostle Peter declared: 'Nor is there salvation in any other; for there is no other name under heaven given among men by which we must be saved' (Acts 4:12).

Joseph did great things to open the storehouses of Egypt: Jesus did far greater things to open the storehouse of salvation

Joseph had to plan and to work diligently for a period of seven years to make sure that the storehouses of Egypt were full. He had to exercise constant oversight.

What did it take for Jesus to open the storehouse of salvation? First, he had to take our humanity. It was humanity that had sinned against God. It was humanity that owed the debt, and it was humanity that would have to pay. As we have noticed so often, Jesus had to be one of us in order to do something for us. This is, of course, what we are celebrating at Christmas. What a wonder! God taking our humanity!

But it wasn't enough for Jesus merely to come in our humanity. He had also to live in perfect obedience to God. If he had committed one sin of his own, he would have had to pay the penalty of eternal destruction for his own sin and would not have been able to pay for the sins of anyone else. And in that humanity he went to the cross. There he received the penalty of eternal wrath in the place of sinners.

All of these things were essential for the storehouse of salvation to be open. And Jesus did them all! And now the storehouse stands open!

That brings us to consider, in the final place, yet another difference between Joseph the saviour and Jesus the Saviour, namely:

Those who came to Joseph had to purchase their grain: those who come to Jesus are given salvation

Salvation cannot be earned or deserved. It is free. The apostle Paul said to the Christians of Ephesus: 'For by grace you have been saved through faith, and that not of yourselves; it is the gift of God, not of works, lest anyone should boast' (Eph. 2:8-9).

But the fact that salvation is a gift does not mean it automatically comes to us. The starving people of Joseph's day 'came to Joseph in Egypt'. And those who are starving spiritually must come to Jesus Christ, acknowledging their desperate condition and asking him for the salvation he came to provide.

Hear his own invitation: 'Come to me, all you who labour and are heavy laden, and I will give you rest' (Matt. 11:28). And hear these words as well: 'And the Spirit and the bride say, "Come!" And let him who hears say "Come!" And let him who thirsts come. And whoever desires, let him take the water of life freely' (Rev. 22:17).

11.
A better kinsman

Read: Ruth 3:9-10, 13-14

The story of Ruth is one of the most gripping and charming in the Bible. If you like romance, you will most certainly like this story. It begins with an Israelite family of four leaving the famine-ravaged land of Israel to reside in Moab. There the husband and father, Elimelech, died. There also the two sons, Mahlon and Chilion, found wives – Ruth and Orpah. After residing there for ten years, Mahlon and Chilion also died, leaving their mother Naomi and their wives. At this point, Naomi decided to leave Moab and return to her home in Israel. And Ruth decided to go with her, speaking these familiar and well-loved words:

> For wherever you go, I will go;
> And wherever you lodge, I will lodge;
> Your people shall be my people,
> And your God, my God.
> Where you die, I will die,
> And there will I be buried.
> (Ruth 1:16b-17a)

It was there in Israel that Ruth met Boaz. The author of Ruth introduces him in this way: 'And Naomi had a kinsman of her husband's, a man of great wealth, of the family of Elimelech; his name was Boaz' (2:1). The word 'kinsman' is key. There were certain laws governing Naomi's situation. And what was her situation? When she returned from Moab, she was probably forced by poverty to sell her deceased husband's property.

The laws that came into play were as follows:

● If a man became impoverished and had to sell his land, it was the right and duty of a near male relative to buy the land. If the nearest kinsman could not or would not do this, the next of kin was given the same opportunity (Leviticus 25:23-28)

● If a man died without children, the nearest male relative was responsible to marry his widow and produce children 'in his name' (Deuteronomy 25:5-10).

Since Naomi herself was past the age of child-bearing, the kinsman that bought the land would also have to marry Ruth, who was essentially part of Naomi's estate, and have children by her. The kinsman himself would not actually come into the possession of the land, but would merely hold it in trust for the son that he and Ruth might produce.

Naomi was well aware of these laws and was most anxious to comply with them. Only by doing so could she secure Ruth's welfare as well as her own. Naomi made a mistake. She assumed that Boaz was her nearest blood relative, but this was not the case. Before he could redeem Naomi's estate and marry Ruth, Boaz had to give the closer relative the opportunity to do these things. When he refused, the way was open for Boaz.

We know how it all turned out. Boaz discharged his responsibilities as the next kinsman. He purchased the property of Naomi and married Ruth. And God blessed their union with a son, Obed, who would become the grandfather of the great king, David.

In order for Boaz to do these things, he had to meet certain qualifications. He had to be a blood relative. He had to have the ability to redeem the inheritance. He had to be willing to redeem the inheritance. And he had to be willing to marry the wife of his deceased kinsman.

Here we are, many centuries later, preparing to celebrate Christmas. I can well understand Mr Average Man, caught up in the rush and crush of it all, wondering what Boaz and Ruth and these ancient customs have to do with him.

I answer by saying that the joy we experience at the Christmas season will be in direct proportion to our understanding of what we are celebrating. The better our understanding, the greater our joy! And part of what we are celebrating at Christmas is this – the Second Person of the Trinity coming to this world to act in the capacity of our kinsman-redeemer.

Furthermore, if we find ourselves admiring what Boaz did as the kinsman-redeemer for Naomi and Ruth, we have even more reason to admire what Jesus did in that capacity. I am asserting that Jesus is a far better kinsman-redeemer than Boaz. How is he superior to Boaz?

The Lord Jesus came to redeem us from a far worse situation than that of Naomi

We can say that we have lost a far greater inheritance than Naomi. She lost her claim to a piece of land in Israel. We have all lost our claim to an eternity of enjoying fellowship with God and sharing his glory. How did we lose such an inheritance? It was through sin.

And now we must do without eternal life or be redeemed from our sin.

We certainly cannot redeem ourselves. We are even more helpless in the spiritual realm than Naomi was in the physical, temporal realm. But, thank God, that does not mean that our lost inheritance is beyond redeeming! The good news of the Bible is that Jesus came to do for us what we could not possibly do for ourselves.

The Lord Jesus had an even greater willingness to redeem

I do not mean to short-change Boaz. He certainly had a willingness to redeem Naomi's estate. Let us give the man the credit he deserves. He did not have to do what he did. He could have passed the opportunity to the next relative, even as the first relative had passed it to him. But Boaz was willing to be the redeemer.

As Boaz was willing to redeem Naomi's estate and marry Ruth, so the Lord Jesus was willing to redeem sinners and make them his holy bride (Eph. 5:23). He did not have to come to this world. Why, then, did he do it? Let the apostle Paul answer: 'For you know the grace of our Lord Jesus Christ, that though he was rich, yet for your sakes he became poor, that you through his poverty might become rich' (2 Cor. 8:9). It was grace! It was not because we earned or deserved it. It was rather because of God's own disposition to love that which is unlovely and to have compassion on that which is totally helpless.

John 3:16 says it perfectly: 'For God so loved the world that he gave his only begotten Son, that whoever believes in him should not perish but have everlasting life.'

We keep wanting to think that God must have seen something in us that made us worthy of him sending his Son, and that Jesus must have seen something in us that made him willing to come. But there was nothing to see except sin and ruin. Any time we look for a reason for redemption outside the heart of God, we are sadly mistaken.

He paid a much higher price to redeem

The price Boaz paid for Naomi's estate was money and marriage! But what a price Jesus paid to redeem sinners!

First, he, the Second Person of the Trinity, took our flesh. The author of Hebrews says of him: 'Inasmuch then as the children have partaken of flesh and blood, he himself likewise shared in the same' (Heb. 2:14). Do we understand these words? We as human beings have sinned, and we must pay the penalty for our sin if we are to regain our lost inheritance. We can put it like this – flesh and blood owes, and flesh and blood must pay.

It would have been a great price indeed if Jesus had done nothing more. But in our flesh he endured terrible hardship and hostility (Heb. 12:3). And in that flesh he went to the cross, where he received the penalty of the eternal wrath of God on our sins. Because Jesus received that penalty and because God only demands that it be paid once, there is no penalty left for those who believe in him.

If Boaz had refused to shoulder the redemption of Naomi's

estate, there would have been another relative willing to do so. But if Jesus had not been willing to redeem us from our sins, there would have been no other redeemer. The work of redemption required one who was fully God and fully man. It was God who was offended by our sins, and it was we who did the offending. For there to be redemption, each party had to be represented. By adding to his deity our humanity, the Lord Jesus was in fact the representative of both parties. But if Jesus, who was fully God, had not been willing to do this, who could then represent God?

This is a day of fascination with angels. People pray to angels, seeking both guidance and protection from them. But no angel can ever redeem us because no angel is God. Let us then make sure that we reserve our worship, praise and faithful service to the only one who is worthy of them – the Lord Jesus Christ!

12.
A better king

Read: Psalm 89:19-29

This psalm was written by Ethan the Ezrahite. The only thing that we know about him is that he wrote these words. At first glance his psalm seems to be about King David of Israel. And, of course, it is. But it is not exclusively about him. We might say that it takes David as its point of departure and rises to a much higher level or to a superior king. It moves from King David to King Jesus. It is what we know of as a messianic psalm.

David was certainly a great king – the greatest of all the kings of Israel. There can be no doubt about that. As we study the kingship of David, we see certain features standing out.

First and foremost, he was obviously a man with a heart for God. The Lord himself refers to David as 'a man after my own heart' (Acts 13:22).

We cannot – we must not! – explain the success of David's reign without making reference to this. His heart for God coloured and influenced everything that he did. Take it away, and you do not have David any longer. To do so would be like taking the brightness from the sun and still calling it the sun. Brightness is the very essence of the sun, and devotion to God was the very essence of King David.

A second feature that stands out about the reign of David is his might as a warrior. It was in this capacity that he burst upon the consciousness of the nation of Israel. As a mere youth, he defeated the Philistine giant, Goliath, with nothing more than a sling and some stones. But his victory over Goliath was only a faint picture of the many victories that would come while he ruled over Israel. David gives testimony to this aspect of his reign in one of his psalms of thanksgiving (2 Sam. 22:35, 38-43). Because of David's success as a warrior, we can move to a third feature of his reign – the expansion of his kingdom. The psalm

68

sets this forth in these words:

> Also I will set his hand over the sea,
> And his right hand over the rivers.
>
> (v.25)

This expansion was such that the reign of David became the first era in which the nation of Israel occupied all of the land that God had promised to give her.

Yet another feature of David's reign was the promise he received regarding the enduring nature of his seed, namely, that he would not fail to have a son sitting on the throne of the nation while there was a nation over which to rule (1 Kings 2:4; 8:25). We are looking at the reign of David at this Christmas season for a very good and sound reason: David points us to an even greater king. That king is, of course, none other than the Lord Jesus Christ.

One aspect of the truth we celebrate at Christmas is the fact that Jesus came to reign over his people. One of our Christmas hymns, 'Come, Thou long-expected Jesus,' puts it in this way:

> *Born Thy people to deliver,*
> *Born a child, and yet a king;*
> *Born to reign in us for ever,*
> *Now Thy gracious kingdom bring.*
>
> (Charles Wesley)

Do we appreciate this aspect of Christ's coming? Are we hailing him as our king? Are we submitting to his rule?

Many resist this truth mightily. They are quite happy with Jesus wrapped in the swaddling clothes and lying in a manger. But King Jesus sitting on the throne of heaven and demanding their allegiance is quite another matter!

My purpose is to show something of the true nature of Christ's kingly reign by comparing it with David's. I am asserting that

Jesus is a far greater king than David. Jesus is the greatest of all kings, and is worthy, therefore, of our allegiance.

Jesus is a greater king because he had a greater devotion to God than David

As we have noticed, David had a genuine devotion to God. But David was not perfect. With that devotion, he was still a deeply flawed man. We all know his story. This man, wonderful as he was, fell into horrible sins. He committed the extremely vile sins of adultery and murder (2 Sam. 11:1-27). This serves as a reminder to us all that even the greatest of men are still sinners. There is only one exception in all of human history, and that is the Lord Jesus Christ. His devotion to God was untainted by sin. There was never a lapse or a lull in it.

While David's life was one of general faithfulness to God, Jesus' life was one of perfect faithfulness to God. He is the only one who truly did 'all' the will of God (Acts 13:22). His life was one of such pristine purity and complete obedience to God that one of his disciples could write of him: 'And you know that he was manifested to take away our sins, and in him there is no sin' (1 John 3:5).

Jesus is superior to David because he defeated greater enemies

David encountered fierce enemies. There is no disputing that. But the enemies he encountered were all flesh and blood. Goliath was awfully big flesh and blood, but still flesh and blood.

In providing salvation for us, the Lord Jesus encountered nothing less than Satan himself and all his minions and forces of evil. Matthew Henry writes: 'He that at first broke the peace would set himself against him that undertook to make peace, and do what he could to blast his design: but he could only reach to bruise his heel.'[3]

---

[3] Matthew Henry, *Matthew Henry's Commentary*, Fleming H. Revell Company, no place, no date, vol. iii, p.577.

Satan is the one who broke the peace between God and men, and Christ is the one who came to restore that peace. The means by which Christ was to restore peace was by his dying on the cross. How Satan tried to divert Jesus from that cross! The night before Jesus died, he said to his disciples: '...the ruler of this world is coming, and he has nothing in me' (John 14:30).

Do we understand what Jesus was saying? Satan was, that very night, coming to make a last-ditch effort to turn him from the cross and thwart the plan of redemption. He was coming to see if there was any unwillingness or hesitation in Jesus about going to the cross. But there was absolutely nothing there with which Satan could work. There was no reluctance or hesitation in Jesus. All Satan could find in him was complete dedication to the task at hand. And, as we know, Jesus went the next day to the cross and there provided salvation for all who believe in him.

As a mighty warrior, he defeated Satan and won the victory. The apostle Paul celebrates the victory by saying of the cross: 'Having disarmed principalities and powers, he made a public spectacle of them, triumphing over them in it' (Col. 2:15).

Look at Psalm 89:22:

> The enemy shall not outwit him,
> Nor the son of wickedness afflict him.

Those words were fulfilled by Jesus. Satan, 'the son of wickedness', could not and did not defeat Jesus! This psalm of Ethan was fulfilled, then, by Jesus.

Jesus is superior to David because his seed endures more than David's seed

The author of this psalm quotes God as saying of Jesus:

> His seed also I will make to endure for ever,
> And his throne as the days of heaven.
>
> (v.29)

Now think about the days of heaven. How many are there?

71

They cannot be counted because there is no end to them. The hymn 'Amazing Grace' presents the day of heaven in this way:

> *When I've been there a thousand years,*
> *Bright shining as the sun,*
> *I've no less days to sing God's praise*
> *Then when I first begun.*
>
> (John Newton)

This is what it means to say Christ has an enduring seed. Those who know him will live with him for ever in heaven. There will be no end to their days.

Jesus' kingship is superior to David's in terms of its scope

As we have noted, David's reign was a time of great expansion for the nation of Israel. But that pales in comparison with the kingdom of Jesus, which is destined to be universally acknowledged. The apostle Paul says of Jesus:

> Therefore God also has highly exalted him and given him the name which is above every name, that at the name of Jesus every knee should bow, of those in heaven, and of those on earth, and of those under the earth, and that every tongue should confess that Jesus Christ is Lord, to the glory of God the Father.
>
> (Phil. 2:9-11)

In other words, a day is coming in which these words will be fulfilled: 'The kingdoms of this world have become the kingdoms of our Lord and of his Christ, and he shall reign for ever and ever!' (Rev. 11:15). As we ponder Jesus, 'the highest of the kings' (Ps. 89:27), we can only say: 'What a king! What a kingdom!' And we must also say: 'How blessed are those who belong to his kingdom!'

Section 4

The treasures
of Christmas

13.
The gift God gave us

Read: John 3:16

A treasure is something we highly value. It is something that is indescribably precious. It doesn't have to have any connection with material wealth. We can treasure a friendship. We can treasure a smile. We can treasure a memory. We can treasure a picture. We can treasure things that others consider to be absolutely worthless and meaningless.

All Christians treasure Christmas. We regard it as being exceedingly precious. We regard it as being of incalculable worth and value. We do so, not for one reason, but for many. We might say, Christians treasure Christmas because it consists of several treasures.

How many treasures are there in Christmas? Who can say? In these weeks that precede Christmas we must be content to look only at four.

The first of these is the gift God gave us. This is the thing we treasure most. This is the very core of Christmas. We celebrate Christmas because God gave us his Son.

This truth is nowhere more powerfully and wonderfully presented than in our text, which is easily the best-loved of all Scripture verses. Martin Luther calls this text 'the Bible in miniature'. R.A. Torrey calls it 'the most wonderful sentence ever written'.[4]

What makes the gift of Christ the most precious of all treasures? He is precious because of:

The incredible need of those to whom he was given

Every Christmas we receive some gifts that we don't really need, but we all need Christ.

---

[4] *Great Pulpit Masters; R.A Torrey*, Fleming H. Revell Company, new York, 1950, vol. iii, p.13

We need him because without him we 'perish'. All we have to do to understand this word is lay it alongside the words 'everlasting life'. Perishing is the exact opposite of everlasting life. It signifies everlasting death or eternal destruction. To perish is to be for ever separated from God, from everything that is good and lovely. It is to miss out on the glories of heaven. It is to experience the wrath of God. There is nothing worse than this. The Bible tells us that we all come into this world facing this terrible peril. Why? The Bible says we are all sinners by nature, and this perishing is the consequence of our sins.

Do we understand that God is holy? That means he cannot compromise with sin. He must judge it. For him to do anything less would be for him to deny himself, which he cannot do. God has to judge sin, and this word 'perish' captures and expresses the judgement of a holy God upon our sins.

The Lord Jesus Christ is the greatest of all Christmas treasures because he, and he alone, can keep us from perishing. He came to this world for the express purpose of making a way for us to be forgiven of our sins.

Christ is also precious because of:

The loving heart that gave him

We cannot walk in this world very long without encountering staggering truths, but there is no more staggering truth than this: 'God so loved the world that he gave his only begotten Son.'

It would be remarkable enough if we were just told that God loves sinners. The thought of God loving people who receive his many good gifts, and yet refuse to acknowledge him and refuse to live according to his laws, is remarkable. But we are told much more than that. God loves sinners so much that he even went so far as to give them his only begotten Son.

God the Father, God the Son, and God the Holy Spirit dwelt in a state of perfect love and fellowship before Jesus ever came. Get this forever etched into your mind and your heart – the triune God did not need fellowship with sinful men. God did not have to lift one finger to redeem sinners. He could have left them in their ruin and been perfectly happy and fulfilled. God did not take up the work of redemption to fill some lack or need. Because he is God, he is perfect in every respect. There is no lack or need in him.

Why, then, did he do it? It was not because of his need, but rather because of our need. He looked upon us in our sin, our misery and our woe. He saw us marching towards eternal destruction. And he was moved with pity and compassion for us, so much so that he sent his Son to this world to redeem us.

Oh, how much it cost God to do this! He saw his Son leave the glories of heaven and come to this earth as a mere baby in little, rude Bethlehem. He saw him living in poverty there in Nazareth. He saw him endure unspeakable hostility and meanness during his earthly ministry. And he saw him go to Calvary's cross and there receive, as he and the Father had planned, the wrath of the holy God against sinners. He saw him spring from the grave on the third day and return to heaven. But he did not come back to heaven in exactly the same state as he was before. No, he came back with our humanity. And he is there now in our humanity as our forerunner (Heb. 6:20). This means that by his very presence there he guarantees that all his people will eventually follow.

What love is this? It is no wonder the poet wrote these lines:

> *The love of God is greater far*
> *Than tongue or pen can ever tell;*
> *It goes beyond the highest star*
> *And reaches to the lowest hell...*
>
> *Could we with ink the ocean fill,*
> *And were the skies of parchment made,*
> *Were every stalk on earth a quill,*
> *And every man a scribe by trade;*
> *To write the love of God above*
> *Would drain the ocean dry;*
> *Nor could the scroll contain the whole*
> *Though stretched from sky to sky.*

Oh, love of God, how rich and pure!
How measureless and strong!
It shall for evermore endure –
The saints' and angels' Song.

(Frederick M. Lehman)

Then again, the gift of Jesus is precious beyond measure because:

It is available to all who believe

Thank God, there is the word 'whoever' in this verse. The gift of God's Son is not only for the rich, the wise, the famous and the powerful. It was not for the Jews only. All of these are invited to come to Christ, but all others are invited as well. You are invited to come to Christ. His redeeming work can count for you. But you must, as John 3:16 so emphatically says, believe in him.

That doesn't mean merely acknowledging certain basic facts about Jesus. I noticed in a recent issue of *The Southern Illinoisian* that readers were invited to respond to the question 'Do you believe Jesus was a real person?' Let us say that an individual responds affirmatively to that inquiry. Does it mean that he is a child of God, that he is saved by the redeeming work of Christ? No, not at all! The book of James tells us that even the very devils of hell have that kind of belief (James 2:19).

Saving belief or saving faith always carries the element of commitment with it. One is saved when he comes to understand his guilt before a holy God, when he renounces all other hopes for forgiveness and rests with complete and final confidence on what Jesus Christ did for sinners. It is saying from the heart the words of the well-known hymn 'Rock of Ages':

Nothing in my hand I bring,
Simply to Thy cross I cling.

(Augustus Montague Toplady)

We will never appreciate the gift of Christ until we see how

78

desperate was our need. But once we understand that, and once we see that Christ was given at tremendous cost to meet it, we will have no trouble laying hold of him in faith, understanding as we do so that he is indeed the greatest of all treasures.

Those who find Christ do not question whether he is the greatest treasure. They rather find themselves bringing their treasures to Christ. The Magi brought gold, frankincense and myrrh. Those who truly know Christ eagerly give to him the treasures of time, talent, energy and, yes, material possessions also.

14.
The card God sent us

Read: Luke 2:8-20

One of the many joys of the Christmas season is receiving cards from family members and friends. The cards I like best are those in which the sender includes a personal note. I find some of these notes to be so meaningful and helpful that I keep them. I have for many years kept a folder labelled 'Special Notes.' When I get discouraged I oftentimes look at those notes. They invariably pick me up. They are part of my treasures.

Have you ever wondered how this practice of exchanging Christmas cards got started? Who came up with the idea? Who sent the first card? And to whom did he or she send it? The answers to these questions may very well be forever concealed in the foggy mists of history.

I cannot identify, in the sense in which we think of Christmas cards, the sender and receiver of the first Christmas card. But I do find something of a Christmas card in the passage before us. There is no envelope or stamp here. There is no Hallmark brand. But all the necessary ingredients of a Christmas card are here. There is a sender (God). There is, as we shall note, a message. There are recipients (shepherds). There is even something of a postman here (the angels). But this card is like no other. It is special.

It is special because it announces a rescue mission

What would you think if you opened a Christmas card to find this message? 'You are in great danger, but there is no need to worry. I am coming to rescue you.' You would think it a very strange card and a very strange sender! But that is essentially what God's Christmas card said. He sent his card by a single angel to some shepherds outside Bethlehem to tell them that he, God, had that very night

80

sent his Son into this world on a rescue mission.

Are you wondering where that is found in the verses before us? It is all right there in that word 'Saviour' (v.11). The angel said: 'For there is born to you this day in the city of David a Saviour, who is Christ the Lord' (v.11). We understand the word 'Saviour'. It means 'deliverer'. A person is about to perish in a burning house, and someone dashes in and carries him to safety. The one who does this is the saviour or the deliverer of the one in the house.

We don't like to hear this these days, but it is still true. We are by nature in great peril. We come into this world with a sinful nature that places us under the wrath of God.

But God in grace sent a Saviour, his Son, the Lord Jesus Christ. He came to be the substitute for sinners. He came to take the wrath of God so that they don't have to experience that wrath themselves. That's what we celebrate at Christmastime. Christmas is nothing less than God's rescue mission. It is God stepping into human history to deliver sinners from the dire consequences of their sins.

We get further insight into this rescue mission from the other titles the angel used for Jesus. He also called him 'Christ' and 'the Lord'. The word 'Christ' means 'anointed One'. It is an official title designating Jesus as the promised Messiah. In the Old Testament, the word 'anointed' is applied to three distinct offices: prophet, priest and king. Jesus' work would reflect each of these offices. In his preaching, he performed the work of the prophet, representing God to men. In his death on the cross, he performed the work of priest, representing men to God. And he is even now at the right hand of the Father, from where he rules and reigns over all those who believe. The word 'Lord' means 'master' or 'exalted one'. Yes, Jesus has been designated and anointed by the Father to be King. But we need to realise that he is Lord over all by virtue of his own person. He is God himself and therefore has authority over all. He has always been Lord. He was Lord before there was ever a plan of redemption and before he was ever designated as the Messiah.

The angel's announcement means there is a very definite and distinct content to the Christmas message. The angel did not say: 'Something marvellous has happened, but just what it is and where it happened is unclear. Try, therefore, to figure it out for yourselves, and that's what Christmas will mean to you.'

No, the angel was specific and definite. A Saviour had been born! The Christ had been born! The Lord had been born! And this was not some kind of vague, ambiguous spiritual experience. He was a real baby and could be found that very moment in Bethlehem.

It is also special because it expresses good will to his enemies

A few of us might find the grace to send a Christmas card to someone we have been at odds with. Some of us might receive such a card. With God's Christmas card we have all received something of this nature. We are by nature the enemies of God (Rom. 5:10; 8:7). Do you doubt this? All you have to do is look at those passages of Scripture that use the word 'reconciliation' (e.g. 2 Cor. 5:18). What are we to understand from this word? What does it mean? It means 'to make peace between enemies'. If God reconciles us to himself, then we must assume that we were at odds with God prior to that reconciliation. This truth of reconciliation to God was, I say, part of the Christmas card God sent the night Jesus was born. The account tells us that after the one angel made his announcement to the shepherds, 'a multitude of the heavenly host' (v.13) appeared to the shepherds saying:

> Glory to God in the highest,
> And on earth peace,
> good will towards men!
>
> (v.14)

No better news can be found! Even though we have rebelled against God, he has good will towards sinners and has made a way in which he can have peace with them.

That way is, of course, his Son, Jesus Christ.

How did Christ make peace between God and sinners? He did so by dealing with sin. Sin is the great cause of separation between man and God. But Christ came to take sin out of the way. The apostle Paul tells us that God reconciles sinners to himself by 'not imputing their trespasses to them' (2 Cor. 5:19). In other words, God saves sinners by not counting their sins against them. But how can a holy God do this? How can he not count sins against sinners? The glorious answer of the Bible is that he accounts those very sins to Jesus Christ instead of to those sinners.

What a wonderful truth this is! Christmas means God has such good will toward sinners that he sent his Son to establish peace between them and himself. No wonder the angels sang: 'Glory to God in the highest'!

It is special because it comes with an RSVP attached

God calls upon each of us to respond to the good news he announced that first Christmas. Yes, that card was delivered to the shepherds, but it was, in the words of the angel, 'to all people' (v.10). The shepherds responded to God's Christmas card. They went to Bethlehem to see the baby (vv.15-16). They shared the good news about that baby with all they met (vv.17-18). And they praised and glorified God for all they had seen and heard (v.20).

How does God want us to respond? He does not want us to undertake a pilgrimage to Bethlehem to see the place Jesus was born. He does not want us to have a warm, sentimental feeling about what happened the night Jesus was born. He does not want us merely to acknowledge that Jesus was born. He wants us to understand that the baby born there that night in Bethlehem came for the express purpose of providing salvation for sinners. He came to Bethlehem's stable so that he might be able to go to Calvary's cross. God wants us to rest ourselves in faith upon the work Jesus did on that cross for sinners.

He also wants a response from those of us who have received

this salvation. He wants us to be gripped with the same spirit of love and compassion that caused him to send the Lord Jesus Christ. He is not pleased when his people walk through this world wearing blinkers. He wants us to be busy telling the gospel story, mending broken hearts and lives and meeting human needs. In other words, he wants all his people to take seriously the words of the apostle Paul: 'Let this mind be in you which was also in Christ Jesus' (Phil. 2:5).

The Lord Jesus came to this world because he had a mind of humble service. We honour him most as our Saviour and Lord when we reflect that same mind.

15.
The tree God
decorated for us

Read: 1 Peter 2:24

The Bible is the story of three trees. The first of these is the tree of the knowledge of good and evil. This is the tree that God placed off-limits for Adam and Eve. His command was for them to refrain from eating of it (Gen. 2:16-17). We can well understand why God would issue this command. Adam and Eve weren't robots. God had made them with true freedom. But freedom is not really freedom if there is no choice to make. So God gave Adam and Eve a choice to make. They could obey him by not eating of the tree of the knowledge of good and evil, or they could disobey by eating from it.

There was yet another tree there in the Garden of Eden. It was the tree of life (Gen. 2:9). It represented eternal life without any possibility of death. My understanding of those early days in the Garden of Eden is that God placed Adam and Eve on probation for a time. If they had successfully passed through this period, he would have given them the privilege of eating of the tree of life. In other words, satisfactory completion of their probation would have led to them receiving eternal life.

The reason God decorated this tree

We know what happened. Adam and Eve refused to obey God. They ate of the first tree and gave up the privilege of eating of the second. This is powerfully and poignantly conveyed to us by the closing words of Genesis 3: 'So he [God] drove out the man; and he placed cherubim at the east of the garden of Eden, and a flaming sword which turned every way, to guard the way to the tree of life' (Gen. 3:24).

The story of the whole human race is wrapped up in the account of Genesis. Man has lost paradise through sin and, left to himself, he can never enter it again. Oh, yes, he tries. How he tries! He tries governmental programmes, education and technology, but he cannot recreate paradise. He tries the hedonistic lifestyle, in which he gives himself over to pleasure and the enjoyment of material possessions. He even tries religion. Yes, sinful man loves religion! The more the better! What he despises is finality in religion, that is, one religion that declares to have the truth of God.

Is there no hope then for sinful men and women? Is there no way they can ever enter paradise again? The good news of the Bible is that there is hope for sinners, that they can indeed re-enter paradise. How is this possible? The answer is in the third tree of the Bible. What tree is this? It is the cross of Jesus Christ, which is quite often called a 'tree' (Acts 5:30; 10:39; Gal. 3:13; 1 Pet. 2:24).

The ornament on this tree

We might say the answer to man's dilemma lies here: God has decorated this tree for us. And what did God use to decorate this tree? There is only one ornament on it, and that is his Son, Jesus Christ.

What an ornament this is! Jesus Christ is hanging on that cross in agony. The blood is streaming down his bruised and battered body. And cruel men are gathered around to hurl their insults and ridicule at him while he hangs there.

Looking on, one would say there is no beauty there. And many these days would wonder how any preacher could dare refer to Jesus Christ as God's ornament on that tree. How is this possible? There is so much ugliness there. There is so much repulsiveness. There is no beautiful ornament there! But, I tell you, there is beauty in that cross! That cross is beautiful by virtue of the One who was suspended on it. He was no ordinary man. He was, as I have already indicated, the very Son of God. He was heaven's brightest treasure, its most resplendent ornament. Before he ever came to this world, he was clothed with the glory of heaven. He shone in unrivalled sovereignty and deity.

How did he come, then, to hang on this cross? What is heaven's brightest ornament doing there? He was there to open heaven's gates to sinners. He was there to free them from the results of their sin. He was there to restore sinners to paradise.

Now here is the great burning question: How, indeed, did Christ's death on that cross open paradise to sinners? Let's revisit the closing words of Genesis 3. There we found access to the tree of life barred by cherubim and a flaming sword. The cherubim form one order of the angels. They are always associated with the holiness of God. The sword, on the other hand, represents God's justice. Those two emblems, the cherubim and the sword, declare powerfully to us that sinful men and women can never again enter paradise until the justice of the holy God against them is satisfied.

This is where the cross of Christ comes in, and this is what makes it so very beautiful. That cross satisfied the justice of the holy God against sinners. That cross is beautiful because it means God found a way to forgive sinners and to bring them into paradise.

Picture it in this way. God is in a great dilemma. His grace stands on one side of his throne, and says to him: 'O God, you are gracious, kind and compassionate. You abound in mercy. You must find a way to forgive sinners their sins. You must make a way for them to enter paradise once again.' And then, from the other side of his throne, his justice speaks to him: 'O God, you must judge sinners. You have promised that the soul that sins shall die. You must keep your word. If you let sinners go free without punishment, you will compromise your holiness and your justice.' The great dilemma before God was, then, how to judge sinners and at the same time let them go free. The dilemma was how to satisfy both the demands of his justice and his grace.

The wisdom of God solved the dilemma. God's wisdom found a way. That way is the cross of Christ. There on the cross Jesus satisfied the demands of God's justice and his grace. He satisfied

God's justice, in that he himself received the penalty for sinners. He stood in their place and received the wrath of God in their stead. Justice stood at the foot of the cross that day and clapped his hands.

On the cross, Jesus also satisfied the grace of God. Because Jesus has taken the penalty for sinners, and because God's justice demands that sin only be punished once, there is no penalty left for believing sinners to pay. With Jesus having paid for their sins they are free to enter paradise. Grace also stood at the foot of the cross and clapped her hands.

The response to God's ornament

The world scorns and ridicules that cross. They hoot at the suggestion that God could use that cross to provide forgiveness for sins and eternal life. Some have even gone so far as to say they could come up with a better plan than that. But those who have received the saving benefit of that cross glory in it. As far as they are concerned, the sceptics can mock and deride. Believers gladly join the apostle Paul in his assessment: 'For the message of the cross is foolishness to those who are perishing, but to us who are being saved it is the power of God... to those who are called... Christ [is] the power of God and the wisdom of God. Because the foolishness of God is wiser than men, and the weakness of God is stronger than men' (1 Cor. 1:18, 24-25).

Because God decorated the tree of Calvary with his Son, Jesus Christ, the Bible promises that all who believe in him will finally enter paradise. The Bible opens with access to the tree of life being denied (Gen. 3:24). It closes with access being restored (Rev. 22:1-2). Those who desire to enjoy this access must repent of their sins and rely completely on the redeeming death of Jesus Christ on the cross.

Those who do so will know the glory of these words:

> *Ten thousand times ten thousand,*
> *In sparkling raiment bright,*
> *The armies of the ransomed saints*
> *Throng up the steeps of light;*

'Tis finished, all is finished,
Their fight with death and sin;
Fling open wide the golden gates,
And let the victors in.

Bring near Thy great salvation,
Thou Lamb for sinners slain;
Fill up the roll of Thine elect,
Then take Thy power and reign;
Appear, Desire of nations,
Thine exiles long for home;
Show in the heaven Thy promised sign;
Thou Prince and Saviour, come!

(Henry Alford)

Man's problem is that he wants paradise without God! He can never get back to paradise as long as he is under the power of Satan. But through Jesus Christ, God's beautiful ornament dying on that cross, God restores sinners to paradise. Christ came to Bethlehem so that he could go to the cross of Calvary. That is the most beautiful of Christmas trees. Christ is the most beautiful of Christmas decorations.

16.
The Christmas feast
God is preparing for us

Read: Revelation 19:6-9

This passage tells us that God is preparing a grand feast for his people. It is called 'the marriage supper of the Lamb' (v.9).

Is it legitimate to call this a Christmas feast? It most assuredly is. Christmas is the celebration of the birth of Jesus, and Jesus came to this earth to 'save his people from their sins' (Matt. 1:21). The culmination of that plan of salvation is that time when the people of God will be gathered home for this marriage supper. Christmas leads to that feast.

The apostle John was given some information to share with us about this feast. He does not tell us all that we would like to know. He only gives us a few titbits, but what tantalising titbits! We can divide his description of it into three parts: the significance of this occasion, the participants in it, and the proper response to it.

The significance of this occasion

This is conveyed by John in these words: 'And I heard, as it were, the voice of a great multitude, as the sound of many waters and as the sound of mighty thunderings' (v.6). This is an event like no other. It is of such importance that it takes a voice like that of a multitude to announce it, a voice so loud that it is comparable to hearing the sound of rushing water and mighty thundering. Why is this such a significant occasion? It proves that the Lord God Omnipotent reigns (v.6).

God has had this wedding in mind from eternity past. It was there that he entered into the covenant of redemption with his Son and with the Holy Spirit. There he gave his Son a people. His plan was that the Son would save those people from their sins and finally bring them into heaven, where they would be joined to him in perfect, intimate and eternal fellowship.

Throughout the running centuries it has often appeared that God's plan would be thwarted and foiled. Wickedness has often seemed so very strong, and the work of God has often seemed to be so very weak. Many times it has appeared that God is not on the throne, that he does not reign, that human events take him by surprise and all is flux and chance. This has been so much the case that Henry Longfellow wrote:

> *I heard the bells on Christmas Day*
> *Their old familiar carols play,*
> *And wild and sweet*
> *The words repeat*
> *Of peace on earth, good-will to men!*
>
> *And in despair I bowed my head:*
> *'There is no peace on earth,' I said,*
> *'For hate is strong,*
> *And mocks the song*
> *Of peace on earth, good-will to men!'*

We are not the first Christians to feel this way. The apostle John was in exile on the isle of Patmos. The leading apostle of the church, Paul, was dead. Christians were being persecuted, and the faith was just creeping along. We might not miss the mark by much if we imagined John being in a state of despondency when he received this book of Revelation. We might even do well to imagine the Lord Jesus giving John a very brief message before giving him the book of Revelation. Perhaps the Lord Jesus said something like this: 'John, I am about to give you a revelation. I want you to write it down and pass it along to the churches. But before I begin I want you to know that we win!'

If that truth was planted in John's mind at the very beginning of this revelation from Christ, it was certainly reinforced by this nineteenth chapter. John hears this tremendously loud voice saying the same thing: 'John, we win!'

Yes, it has often looked as if the cause of God was hastening to defeat. Yes, it has often looked as if Satan was reigning and God was frustrated. But the truth of the matter is that, in all the twists and turns of human history, God has been reigning. He has been working his purposes out, and he has been working them out with such precision and such power that finally he will achieve exactly what he set out to achieve. He is going to give his redeemed people to his Son!

This is a significant occasion, then, because it proves that our God has been reigning all along.

The participants in this occasion

There cannot be a marriage feast without a groom and a bride, and in this vision John sees both. The groom is, of course, the Lord Jesus Christ, and the bride is his church. We should note that the groom is here identified as the Lamb (v.7). Why is Christ called a Lamb? Several animals were used for sacrifice in the Old Testament, but no animal is more associated with sacrifice than the lamb. That association is primarily due to the Passover, one of the key events of the Old Testament.

God promised to deliver the people of Israel from their bondage in Egypt by bringing severe judgement upon Pharaoh and the Egyptians. This judgement would come in the form of God's angel of death passing over the land of Egypt to slay the firstborn in every family. The Israelites would be spared this judgement by marking their doors with the blood of a lamb. All who were in these houses would be safe. The angel of death would pass over them. In effect, the lamb died in the place of those people (Exodus 12:1-30).

All of this foreshadowed the work of the Lord Jesus Christ. He came to be the Lamb of God, to be the substitute for sinners. He came to receive the penalty of their sin. By virtue of coming in the capacity of a lamb and dying for his people, the Lord Jesus frees them from their sins and makes them his bride. Samuel J. Stone writes of the Lord Jesus and his church:

> *From heaven He came and sought her*
> *To be His holy bride;*
> *With His own blood he bought her,*
> *And for her life He died.*

As we turn our attention to the bride, we find John focusing on her attire: 'to her it was granted to be arrayed in fine linen, clean and bright, for the fine linen represents the righteous acts of the saints' (v.8). This verse has sparked debate over the nature of this righteousness. Is it the righteousness of Christ that is imputed to believers in salvation? Or is it the practical acts of righteousness that these believers perform as they serve the Lord? The text indicates the latter, but that doesn't completely exclude the former. Christians do righteous acts because they have received the former. Receiving the righteousness of Jesus Christ fills believers with the desire to practise righteousness.

We must not leave the subject of the bride's attire without noticing that she only possesses it because of the grace of God. John says 'to her it was granted to be arrayed'. The bride can take absolutely no credit at all for her salvation. It is all due to God working in her.

The proper response to this occasion

How should we respond to all this? There is a proper response from believers and a proper response from unbelievers.

First, believers, as those who have been redeemed by the grace of God, should 'be glad and rejoice and give him glory' (v.7). John focuses our attention on the blessedness of the redeemed with these words: 'Blessed are those who are called to the marriage supper of the Lamb!' (v.9). No greater privilege can be bestowed upon a mere mortal than this – being one of the redeemed who make up the church. Nothing approaches this! How thankful we should be!

If we understand the greatness of this privilege, we will be expressing our thanks to God. We will be regularly engaging in public worship. We will be constantly seeking to obey his commands. We will be seeking opportunities to spread the word about what he has done for us.

What about those who are not believers, those who have not received the Lord Jesus Christ? How should they respond to the truth of this approaching marriage feast? The proper response of the unbeliever is to make sure that he is included in this great marriage feast. Whatever else one fails to do, he must not fail here! How does one gain access to the marriage feast? He must repent of his sins and rest his hopes for eternal life completely on what Jesus did for sinners.

We have in the Gospel of Matthew a parable from the Lord Jesus about this very matter. A king provided a marriage feast for his son. When the guests arrived, the king came out to greet them. He immediately noticed a man who was not wearing the wedding garment that he, the king, had provided. He confronted that man with these words: 'Friend, how did you come in here without a wedding garment?' There was nothing for the man to say by way of defence, and the king had his servants bind him hand and foot and cast him into a place of darkness, weeping and gnashing of teeth (Matt. 22:1-14).

To be included in the wedding feast of Christ, you must be attired in the garment that God himself provides through the redeeming work of his Son, the garment of perfect righteousness. You may fancy that you will sneak in unnoticed. You may imagine that if anyone notices, you will be excused by merely saying, 'My own clothes are good enough.' But such thoughts will prove to be vain. No one will go unnoticed and no garment will be accepted except the one provided by God. If you are not yet clothed in it, put it on today by repenting of your sins and trusting Christ as your Saviour. Christmas is a delight for those who will be at the feast God is preparing.

Section 5

Questions answered by Christmas

17.
Does God exist?

One of the many joys and delights of Christmas is the answers it gives to life's most important questions.

No question is of more importance than the one before us. If there is no God, Christianity is clearly mistaken, and if Christianity is mistaken, everything changes. If there is no God, we are not his creatures, and we are not under his authority. If there is no God, there is no Judge before whom we must stand. If there is no God, there are no sinners, and, therefore, no need for forgiveness of sins. If there is no God, there is no eternal destruction and no eternal life.

Many go through all of life without having any certainty about whether God exists. All such would do well to think long and hard about Christmas. It tells us that there is no need to be in doubt about this matter. Christmas affirms the existence of God in a remarkable and powerful way.

The event of Christmas proves the existence of God

By the event of Christmas, I am referring to the birth of Christ. The day of his birth was the first Christmas. As we examine that blessed event, we can quite easily find certain realities that infallibly point to the existence of God.

Supernatural activities

For one thing, the first Christmas featured a burst of activities that can only be considered supernatural. Angels appeared to Joseph (Matt. 1:20), Zacharias (Luke 1:11-13), Mary (Luke 1:26-38) and to the shepherds outside Bethlehem (Luke 2:8-15). An unusual star appeared in the east to the wise men, and again when they arrived in Jerusalem (Matt. 2:2, 9-10). These same men were also 'divinely warned in a dream' that they should not return to Herod to report to him their encounter with the young child (Matt. 2:12).

The greatest of all these supernatural occurrences was, of course, the birth itself. Scripture affirms that Jesus' birth was like no other. He was conceived by the Holy Spirit and born of a virgin (Matt. 1:20-25). To accomplish this, the laws of nature had to be suspended, and this is something that God alone can do.

The virgin birth has been much disputed, but the evidence for it is incontrovertible. Two of the Gospel writers, Matthew and Luke, affirm it. It is important to remember that these Gospels were written only a few years after Jesus' death and resurrection. Many of those most closely associated with Jesus were still alive when these Gospels began to circulate. We may rest assured that these people would have quickly set the record straight if the accounts of Matthew and Luke were not true. Mary herself was still alive when these Gospels were written. She would most certainly have denied these accounts if they were not true. Luke's account of the virgin birth is especially noteworthy because of his profession as a physician. He would have been naturally sceptical of such a thing, but after careful research (Luke 1:1-4), it is he who gives the fuller account of it (Luke 1:26-38).

Supernatural control
In addition to these things, we must also say that the first Christmas featured a God-like control of events.

Centuries before Jesus was born, the prophet Micah had announced that Bethlehem would the place of the Messiah's birth (Micah 5:2). Now consider the things that 'fell into place' when Jesus was born. Caesar Augustus, who probably did not even know where Bethlehem was, issued a decree that required everyone to go to their home towns (Luke 2:1-3). That decree made it necessary for Joseph and Mary to go to Bethlehem, and while they were there, her pregnancy came to full term. Some will chalk all this up to coincidence, but when a situation requires lots of coincidences, one cannot help but see the hand of God at work.

God's control of events surrounding the birth of Jesus extends beyond those things we have just noticed. The apostle Paul says

Jesus was born 'when the fullness of the time had come' (Gal. 4:4). When Jesus was born, the world was ripe for his coming.

There was a prevalent language, Greek, in which the gospel could be preached. There was a road system, which gave preachers of the gospel access to many regions. And there was a spiritual vacuum in the hearts of the people. Jesus came after Jewish religion, Greek philosophy and the Roman government had all failed to satisfy the deepest longings of the human heart. This is all clear evidence of God at work, controlling history and bending it to suit his purpose.

Let's now turn our attention to the second major proof that Christmas furnishes for the existence of God:

The Christ of Christmas proves the existence of God

Those who doubt the existence of God must find some way to explain Jesus. If he was God in human flesh, there has to be a God. Jesus could not have been God in human flesh if there is no God!

Jesus certainly claimed to be God in human flesh. He claimed to be sent from God (John 7:28-29; 8:42), to exercise the prerogatives of God (John 5:21-23, 25-27), to do the works of God (John 10:37-38) and to speak for God (John 12:49-50). In addition to all these things, Jesus categorically stated that he was God. On the night before he was crucified, he said to his disciples: 'He who has seen me has seen the Father (John 14:9). The apostles also strongly affirmed that Jesus was God in human flesh (John 1:14, 18; 2 Cor. 5:19). Are the claims of Jesus and his apostles true? Is there evidence to support them? Was Jesus really God in human flesh?

There are many evidences that he was. One is fulfilled prophecy, an evidence we shall consider in the next chapter.

There is also the evidence supplied by the miracles that he performed. These miracles cannot be easily dismissed or explained away. They were great in number. Jesus healed the sick, cast out demons, raised the dead, stilled storms and fed multitudes. They were, as one glance quickly reveals, also of various types. Jesus did not just do one kind of miracle again and again. And these miracles were also witnessed by multitudes. They were not like the solitary golfer claiming a hole-in-one!

The single most convincing evidence that Jesus was indeed God in human flesh is his own resurrection from the grave. The resurrection itself is one of the best-attested events in all of ancient history. The heavy stone sealing the tomb was moved (Matt. 28:2; Mark 16:3-4; Luke 24:2). Jesus' body was missing (Matt. 28:5-6; Luke 24:3). Angels were present (Matt. 28:2-5; Mark 16:5-7; Luke 24:4-6). The grave clothes were left in a convincing configuration (Luke 24:12; John 20:6-7). The risen Lord appeared to many (Acts 1:3; 1 Cor. 15:1-8) and the cowering disciples of Jesus were transformed into bold witnesses (Acts 4:13; 5:22-32).

There was no doubt in the mind of the apostle Paul about the significance of Jesus' resurrection. He says that Jesus was 'declared to be the Son of God with power by the resurrection from the dead' (Rom. 1:4). Paul's words are very interesting. He does not say that Jesus was 'made' the Son of God by his resurrection, but rather that he was 'declared' by the resurrection to be the Son of God. Jesus could not be made the Son of God because he always was God and never ceased to be. The resurrection simply declared him to be what he had been all along.

The event of Christmas and the Christ of Christmas give us irrefutable evidence that God does indeed exist. But God is not satisfied with us merely acknowledging his existence. We can do nothing else until we acknowledge that, but we must not be content to do nothing more. We will do no better than the devils of hell if we merely believe in the existence of God (James 2:19). We only surpass the demons if we come to God in repentance of our sins and in faith in Christ. God sent his Son to this world to provide the way of salvation for sinners. That is the reason for Christmas. And we can never be acceptable to God apart from the redeeming work of Christ.

18.
Can God be trusted?

Read: Luke 1:54-55, 68-80

One of the things for which our times will most be known is gambling. There has been a gambling explosion in the last several years. Casinos and lotteries abound on every hand as people squander their earnings, and even savings, on the hope of striking it rich.

While this type of gambling is very damaging indeed, it pales in comparison to that which can be called spiritual gambling. Untold millions are engaging in this deadly business. They are gambling with their eternal well-being.

We have in Scripture a message that claims to be from God. This is at one and the same time a disturbing and cheering message. It is disturbing in that it tells us that we are all sinners and that we must eventually give account of ourselves to God. It is a cheering message in that it tells us that God, in and through his Son, Jesus Christ, has done everything necessary for our sins to be forgiven so we can stand acceptably before him.

Many reject this message. They are gambling everything on the hope that this message is false and unreliable.

Are these spiritual gamblers correct? Is the message of the Bible unreliable or is it true? The Bible claims God as its ultimate author. To ask if the Bible is reliable is, then, the same as asking if God himself can be trusted.

Many promises fulfilled

We need not be in suspense about this matter. Christmas gives us a clear and definitive word about it. The birth of Jesus in Bethlehem constituted a resounding and triumphant 'Yes!' to the question 'Can God be trusted?' It was the fulfilment of many promises from God over the period of many centuries.

Fulfilment was much on the minds of Mary and Zacharias when they learned that the Messiah was about to be born. Mary glorified God for remembering the mercy that he had promised when he spoke to Israel's fathers (Luke 1:46-55). Zacharias offered praise to God for fulfilling what he had spoken 'by the mouth of his holy prophets, who have been since the world began' (Luke 1:67-79).

Zacharias' words indicate that God's promise to send the Messiah goes back to the very beginning of time. Indeed it does. God first gave the promise to Adam and Eve after they fell into sin in the Garden of Eden. He promised that one born of a woman would eventually deal Satan a crushing blow (Gen. 3:15). This was nothing less than a prophecy of the Messiah himself.

From that first statement we find in the Old Testament an ever-widening stream of promises regarding the coming Messiah. Jacob spoke of the Messiah as the 'Shiloh' (peaceful one) who would spring from the tribe of Judah (Gen. 49:10). Balaam spoke of him as the Star that would arise from Jacob and the sceptre out of Israel (Num. 24:17). Moses spoke of him as the Prophet who would come with God's words in his mouth (Deut. 18:15-18). The prophet Isaiah spoke of him as Wonderful, Counsellor, the Mighty God, the Everlasting Father and the Prince of Peace (Isa. 9:6). Jeremiah spoke of him as the Branch of righteousness who would 'execute judgment and righteousness in the earth' (Jer. 33:15). Micah spoke of him as the one 'whose goings forth have been from of old, from everlasting', and prophesied that he would be born in Bethlehem (Micah 5:2).

In addition to giving these and many, many more promises, the Lord also gave throughout the Old Testament era certain types or pictures of the coming Christ. These types may be divided into three categories: persons, events and institutions. Some of the Old Testament individuals who served as types of the coming Messiah were Joseph and David. An event that pictured Christ was Noah's building of the ark to save his family from the flood. And the institution that most readily comes to mind as a type of

Christ is the sacrificial system.

All of these things lead us to conclude that the Old Testament is full of Christ. We know that the Lord Jesus regarded the Old Testament in this way. On the day of his resurrection, he walked along the road to Emmaus with two of his disciples, and 'expounded to them in all the Scriptures the things concerning himself' (Luke 24:27).

That same evening, he spoke these words to his disciples in Jerusalem: 'These are the words which I spoke to you while I was still with you, that all things must be fulfilled which were written in the Law of Moses and the Prophets and the Psalms concerning me' (Luke 24:44). We are further told that he 'opened their understanding, that they might comprehend the Scriptures' (Luke 24:45).

Many challenges conquered

Christians emphatically assert that the Lord Jesus Christ fulfilled the Old Testament prophecies and types. Most are so familiar with the assertion that they are not at all surprised when they hear it. The thing that often escapes notice is how many times it seemed as if the promise of the Messiah would not be fulfilled. One of these promises was that the Messiah would spring from David's line. What is so remarkable about that? The answer is that there were times when it looked as if David would not even have a line. The evil Athaliah set out to destroy all his heirs and would have succeeded had not Jehosheba taken measures to hide Joash (2 Kings 11:2-3; 2 Chron. 22:10-12).

Then there was that time when the whole nation of Judah was carried into captivity in Babylon. At that time the very existence of the nation itself seemed to be very much in doubt. How could the promises of a Messiah be fulfilled if the nation to whom the Messiah had been promised did not exist?

Of course, we know how it all turned out. We know that the promises of God, no matter how imperilled they appeared to be, never came close to failing because they were guaranteed by the one who cannot fail. The Messiah not only came to this earth, but also came at the exact time that God had foreordained (Gal. 4:4).

The faithfulness of God to his promises is such that Joshua was able to speak these words to the nation of Israel: 'And you know in all your hearts and in all your souls that not one thing has failed of all the good things which the Lord your God spoke concerning you. All have come to pass for you, and not one word of them has failed' (Josh. 23:14).

So what?

What does all this have to do with us? The answer is quite simple. We have in Scripture the message of God. It is, as we have noted, a message about our sins and guilt before God and of forgiveness through Christ. It is a message about the glories that await the children of God in heaven and the destruction that awaits those who reject it. If this message is false, we can safely ignore it and live our lives as we please. But if is true, it is utter folly to reject it.

Some suggest that there is no way to tell whether the message is true, that one person's guess is just as good as another's. The first Christmas proved beyond dispute that God can be trusted. He spoke throughout the Old Testament period, and what he spoke was fulfilled to the letter.

If God has been so faithful to his word in the past, it is only logical to believe that he will continue to be faithful. Those who are gambling their eternal destiny on the unreliability of God's message will some day find, as all gamblers eventually do, how terribly mistaken they were. But it will then be too late to change course.

Christmas pleads with all these to understand the reliability of God's Word and to act on it now by repenting of their sins and receiving the Lord Jesus Christ as their Lord and Saviour.

19.
Can we know God?

Read: 1 John 5:11-13, 20

Every Christmas we hear all kinds of statements about what Christmas is 'all about'. One says: 'Christmas is all about family.' Another says: 'Christmas is all about giving.' Still another adds: 'Christmas is all about loving.' While we certainly understand the sentiments behind these statements, we must say that they fall short of the essential meaning of Christmas.

What, then, is Christmas really 'all about?' I can put it in these words: Christmas means Christ came, and Christ came so that sinners could know God.

The apostle John affirms this in these words: 'And we know that the Son of God has come and has given us an understanding, that we may know him who is true' (1 John 5:20). In these words to his fellow Christians, the apostle John binds Christmas and the knowledge of God together. He says, 'the Son of God has come [there's Christmas] … that we may know him who is true [there's the knowledge of God]'.

To the one who asks if it is possible to know God, Christmas offers an emphatic and triumphant 'Yes!'

Consider, then, some of the major aspects of knowing God.

It is an exhilarating business

When we talk about knowing God, we speak of the purpose for which he made us. The first man and woman, Adam and Eve, were made by God, and they knew God.

There are, as we know, different levels of knowledge of others. First, there is the awareness level. We know millions and millions of people in this way. We have no personal knowledge of them, but we know they exist. Then there is the acquaintance level. We have this type of relationship with many. We may not know their names, but we know we have seen them before, and we speak to them and they to us. Then there is the friendship category. We are much better acquainted with those in this group. We have a personal knowledge of them and varying degrees of knowledge about them. Finally, there is the intimate category. We know what makes the people in this group tick. We know something of their desires, motives, misgivings, strengths, weaknesses and fears.

It is in this category that we must place Adam and Eve's knowledge of God. They were not just aware of God or casually acquainted with him. They were more than just friends with him. They had a deep and intimate knowledge of him. They were conscious of his presence. They gave him priority. They knew his ways. They partook of his character. They magnified his worth. They desired communion with him. They enjoyed his fellowship as he walked with them day after day in the beautiful Garden of Eden.

Nothing is so satisfying as realising the purpose for which we have been made, and for a while Adam and Eve lived very happy and satisfying lives. Imagine it! Walking with the God who made them! Fellowshipping with the God who is unlimited in power and wisdom, who is clothed in majesty and splendour that are inexpressible! Communing with the God who is gracious and kind beyond description! What privileges Adam and Eve enjoyed!

Then one day it all changed. They disobeyed the only commandment that the Lord had given them, and their fellowship with him and enjoyment of him were broken. The Lord came to walk with Adam and Eve, and, instead of welcoming him and enjoying his presence, they hid from him (Gen. 3:8-10).

The exhilaration of knowing God had been replaced by the misery of being alienated from him.

It is essential business

The sin of Adam and Eve, in and of itself, would have

106

been incredibly sad, but the tragedy of it extended far beyond them to include all of us. Adam was our representative head. What he did counted for us!

This means, therefore, that we all come into this world, not in the fellowship with God that Adam and Eve enjoyed at first, but rather with a nature that is opposed to him and is set on gratifying itself. The news gets worse. Because we are out of fellowship with God in this life, we are destined to be out of fellowship with him for ever. The greatest question of the ages, then, is how can sinful men and women be restored to fellowship with God?

Our reading answers this question with plainness. It affirms that Jesus Christ is the way back into fellowship with, or knowledge of, God.

It is a very precise business

It is achieved in a very definite and distinct way, and that way is Jesus. The apostle John powerfully makes this point: 'And this is the testimony: that God has given us eternal life, and this life is in his Son. He who has the Son has life; he who does not have the Son of God does not have life' (1 John 5:11-12). The Lord Jesus himself put it in these words: 'I am the way, the truth, and the life. No one comes to the Father except through me' (John 14:6).

Nothing about the Christian message so upsets and disturbs modern hearers as its emphasis on precision. We like precision in other areas of life, but we have a tendency to dislike it in this matter of knowing God. We would be appalled if a doctor were to practise imprecise surgery. We want him to be very, very precise! But when it comes to the things of God, we are inclined to think that all religions, all beliefs, all opinions are equally valid, and that no one has the right to say one belief is superior. Why do we say that Jesus alone is the way for sinners to come to the true knowledge of God and fellowship with him? Why is one way not as good as another when it comes to this matter? The short answer is because God wants it that way! We are prone to think God should bow to our notions of political correctness, but he is under no obligation to do so. He is the one who has been offended by our sin. He is the one who must be appeased before he will allow us to enter into his heaven. He is the one who came up with the idea of salvation. He is the one who desired to save sinners and to share heaven with them. He is the one who formulated the plan of salvation. He did not have to do anything at all to save us, and we should not, therefore, object to any plan of salvation that he adopts.

As we look at the plan of salvation God actually constructed, we can see the wisdom of it and why it has to be the way it is. Not just any plan of salvation will do. The penalty for sin is eternal separation from God, and that penalty must be paid by either the sinner himself of by someone who stands as his substitute or surety.

It was necessary for the Son to take our humanity so he could stand in our place and pay our penalty. On the cross, the Lord Jesus paid that penalty. He actually experienced the wrath of God against sinners. Because he was the God-man, he could suffer in a finite amount of time an infinite amount of wrath. On that cross, the billows of God's wrath rolled over him. He experienced the pangs of hell so that those who believe in him will never have to experience those same pangs. Because Jesus alone did this, he alone is the way for us to be forgiven of our sins and to be brought back into fellowship with God.

It is also urgent business
If Jesus is the only way of salvation, it is crucial that we repent of our sins and accept him as our Lord and Saviour. Nothing is of more critical importance.

This matter is also urgent because this life so swiftly passes. Life at its very longest is very short. The wind of time propels us with terrific speed through life, and we land in eternity. Only those who know God through the Lord Jesus Christ land safely. Whatever else we fail to do in this life, we must not fail to prepare for eternity. Christ came to ensure that those who believe in him will land safely there, and that is what Christmas is really all about.